CROSSOVER CREATIVITY

Also by Dave Trott

Creative Mischief
Predatory Thinking
One Plus One Equals Three: A Masterclass in Creative Thinking
Creative Blindness (And How To Cure It)
The Power of Ignorance

CROSSOVER CREATIVITY

REAL-LIFE STORIES ABOUT WHERE CREATIVITY COMES FROM

Dave Trott

HARRIMAN HOUSE LTD
3 Viceroy Court
Bedford Road
Petersfield
Hampshire
GU32 3LJ
GREAT BRITAIN
Tel: +44 (0)1730 233870

Email: enquiries@harriman-house.com
Website: harriman.house

First published in 2023.
Copyright © Dave Trott

Paperback ISBN: 978-0-85719-988-1
eBook ISBN: 978-0-85719-989-8

British Library Cataloguing in Publication Data
A CIP catalogue record for this book can be obtained from the British Library.

CONTENTS

CONTENTS

Every owner of a physical copy of this edition of

Crossover Creativity

can download the eBook for free direct from us at
Harriman House, in a DRM-free format that can be
read on any eReader, tablet or smartphone.

Simply head to:

ebooks.harriman-house.com/crossovercreativity

to get your copy now.

ABOUT THE AUTHOR

Dave Trott is a creative director, copywriter, and author. He studied at the Pratt Institute in New York City, majoring in advertising before going on to found the advertising agencies Gold Greenlees Trott, Bainsfair Sharkey Trott and Walsh Trott Chick Smith. In 2004 he was given the D&AD President's Award for lifetime achievement in advertising. He has also received lifetime achievement in advertising awards from The Creative Circle, The Marketing Society, and the Scottish Advertising Association.

Dave is married with two children and lives in London. *Crossover Creativity* is his sixth book.

INTRODUCTION

Consider a Venn diagram – either extreme on its own is boring, ordinary, predictable.

But move the two extremes together, so they overlap where they meet.

The overlap is the creative part, the electricity, that is where the magic happens: that's where two disconnected things form a third thing, a *new* thing.

The overlap didn't even exist until two unrelated things came together.

Then something springs into existence, something no one saw before.

That's crossover creativity.

That's what this book is about, putting things together.

Comparing and contrasting, collating and judging, seeking input and provocations.

Because that's what makes ideas.

To do that we need lots of input, and we need lots of differing perspectives:

Like crossing a hit music studio with an automobile production line.

Like using barbed wire to make phone calls.

Like comparing elephants to violent teenagers.

Like training soldiers via erotic comic books.

Like faking your own death for self-promotion.

Like getting a driver drunk to win a race.

Like turning the predator into the prey.

Like renaming a fish to make it taste delicious.

Like reporting on a football match in ancient Greek.

Like getting your main competitor to sell your product for you.

Like driving an F1 car in neutral to win a Grand Prix.

Like exchanging a paperclip for a house.

Like raising a million dollars by asking for a dime.

Like paying for fighter pilots to change sex.

Like buying books you couldn't even see or read.

Like rewriting basic numbers as an emotional, moving story.

Like paying for a fake painting with fake money.

Like using knitting, tin cups, even blinking to communicate.

Like editing the Bible with a razor blade to reveal the inner truth.

From all that, we can see that ideas don't just come out of nowhere.

Two things come together and a third thing happens.

Because new ideas are actually a reaction when existing things cross over.

They are the product of *recombinant thinking*.

All we have to do is keep putting things together and see how they react.

The more things we put together the more reactions we get.

The more reactions we get, the more ideas we'll have.

All we have to do is collect lots of different, unconnected things to put together.

That's crossover creativity.

PART 1

LETTING IDEAS IN

THIS ISN'T AN EXAM

In 1953, a young man left the army and got a job at Ford's factory in Detroit.

He didn't want to work on the production line all his life, so he began writing songs.

Some were hits, so he quit his day job and began writing songs full time.

But he didn't want to lose control of the songs when they were recorded.

So he thought bigger, he began producing the recordings himself and selling his recordings to bigger labels to publish.

Which made him think, why don't I have my own label and publish them myself?

So, in 1959, he began publishing songs on his own label.

Which meant he could attract lots of young artists.

Which meant he could afford to turn his house into a recording studio.

Which meant he controlled the whole process, beginning to end.

But then he thought even bigger.

And this is where he put what he'd learned at Ford's production line together with the music business.

He'd seen the bare chassis of a car start at the beginning, then have the various components added: engine, transmission, seats, bodywork, wheels, windows, until by the end it was a complete, beautiful, finished car.

And that's what he wanted his artists to be: not just singers but complete entertainers.

He started with the raw talent, but he didn't just want voices people would listen to on records.

He wanted polished entertainers that people would pay to see perform.

So, like the production line, he added the parts as they went along.

He started with good singers, but then he had Maurice King, as Musical Director of Artistic Development, add sophistication and class to the artists.

He taught them how to project, how to phrase, how to blend, he arranged their music.

Then Cholly Atkins was added, to teach them stage presence.

So they didn't just stand and sing, or sit and sing, they had a complete choreographed performance with every song.

And as a finishing touch, Maxine Powell was added, to teach them dress and style and etiquette.

They learned to perform and speak and talk and even eat with elegance, so they would be at ease at the White House or Buckingham Palace.

And when the artists were rolling off the production line, just like at Ford, they were the finished complete product, unlike any other companies' artists.

His record label employed 450 people, and had 110 top ten hits between 1960 and 1970.

The young man's name was Berry Gordy, and the record label he founded was Motown.

Some of the artists to roll off his production line are as follows:

Smokey Robinson & The Miracles, Diana Ross & The Supremes, Michael Jackson & The Jackson Five, The Four Tops, The Temptations, Marvin Gaye, Stevie Wonder, Lionel Richie, Tammi Terrell, Gladys Knight & The Pips, Al Green, The Isley Brothers, Mary Wilson, Eddie Kendricks, The Commodores, Junior Walker, The Pointer Sisters, Edwin Starr, and lots more.

All by ignoring the rules of the music business and making up his own rules.

By using what he'd learned from a completely different business, the production line at Ford, and applying it to the music business.

He didn't try to do the music business the way everyone said it should be done.

But I often think that's how we do our jobs.

Frightened to step out of line in case anyone points the finger at us.

Frightened of not doing it the way everyone else agrees it should be done.

We are so worried about getting every little detail approved we forget to be exciting.

I think we forget this isn't school, this isn't university, this isn't an exam.

ANOTHER GLASS OF WINE?

Most of us have different types of wine glasses at home – why is that?

If asked, we'll probably say we need different glasses for different kinds of wine.

We might say red wine needs a wider glass for the fuller aroma, white wine needs a smaller, narrower glass for the more delicate flavour.

That's what we honestly believe about different sorts of glasses.

That the shapes have evolved over time, and people always drank different wines from the best glasses for that particular wine.

But that's not the truth – it's clever marketing.

We can learn a lot from Austrian glassmaker, Claus Riedel.

Because, unlike most marketing people, he understood the difference between talking to **'Triallists'** and talking to **'Current Users'**.

Most of us kneejerk into talking to 'Triallists' without giving it a second's thought.

We list what's good about our brand or product and look for new consumers, people who haven't tried it yet.

But what if the market has reached saturation, especially with a consumer durable: something people don't buy often?

How do you grow a market where everyone already has what you make and doesn't need any more of it?

Claus Riedel was the first person to see an opportunity in talking to that market.

Until the 1950s, most people had just one set of glasses and they used them for whatever drinks guests wanted: white wine, red wine, etc.

Claus Riedel was the first to introduce the concept of different glasses for different wines.

He said a single set won't do, you can't serve different wines from the same glasses.

So, in 1958 he launched the Burgundy Grand Cru glass at The Brussels World Fair.

It was designed to **"enhance the flavours and aromas of the Pinot Noir and Nebbiolo grape variety, specifically for Burgundy, Barolo, and Barbaresco wines"**.

A glass made specially for a particular wine was a totally new concept.

It won the Gold Medal and was acquired by the Museum of Modern Art in New York.

Then, in 1961 Riedel introduced the first full line of wine glasses created for different wines.

And, in 1973 Riedel introduced the Sommeliers Series, the world's first gourmet glasses.

Now, on Riedel's website it says: **"Claus Riedel is best known for creating grape variety-specific glassware designed to enhance types of wine based on specific properties of individual grape varieties. He was among the first glassware experts in history to recognise that the taste of wine is affected by the shape of the glass, and is credited with first discovering and developing variety-specific glassware shapes and bringing these glasses to the consumer market."**

Riedel was in charge of the family company that had been in business since 1756.

It must have been very hard to give up being a glassware company to become a specialist 'wine glass company' especially as different wine glasses didn't even exist.

But Riedel saw it as an opportunity to stop competing with every other glassware company.

If he could make people want different wine glasses, he'd have that market to himself.

But first, he would have to build the market for different wine glasses.

He'd have to sell different types of glasses to people who thought one set was enough.

He'd have to explain why one set wasn't nearly enough.

People love to believe wine is esoteric, so the more inscrutable he could make it, the better.

Claus Riedel grew the market by adding a whole new level of complexity.

By allowing people to demonstrate being part of the cognoscenti.

He built a brand-new market on the back of the glass market that existed, by reinventing wine drinking.

And that is genuine creative thinking.

OLD TECH v NEW TECH

In 1970, John Seely Brown (JSB) was professor of Advanced Computing Science (specialising in A.I.) at the University of California.

He was fascinated by Xerox PARC (Palo Alto Research Center) where all the most forward-thinking computer developments were happening.

But while PARC was inventing the future, it just wasn't connecting with the public.

Computers were still seen as dry and technical, only for a few specialised professionals.

JSB was thinking about this as he spoke to PARC's founder and chief scientist, Jack Goldman.

After they discussed PARC and the future, Goldman asked if JSB had any questions.

JSB said: **"Just the one Jack, how come you have two telephones on your desk?"**

Goldman said: **"Well this is the old one I've always had. This other one is the new one we all have to have. It's got every function possible but it's so complicated I don't have time to learn how to use it. So when it's an important call, I just use the old one."**

And that's when the light went on in JSB's head.

The difference between those *making* the technology, and those who should be *using* it.

Even the chief scientist at PARC couldn't be bothered to learn the new technology.

And JSB realised they had it the wrong way round, they were trying to make new technology dictate to people.

But, just like economics, it doesn't work that way.

They were trying to make supply dictate demand when, in fact, demand dictates supply.

So JSB began to introduce anthropologists, sociologists, and psychologists into the process.

Scientists who could think about the people the technology was *supposed* to be for.

By ignoring those people they had been over-complicating simple things.

At this time, Xerox's main income came from copiers in virtually every office in America.

When there was a problem with a copier, Xerox sent a technician to fix it.

These visits were time-consuming, and customers were unhappy because the copier was offline while the technician located the problem.

But Xerox did have one technician who was really fast and popular with his customers.

In fact, the technician had become known as **'Mr Troubleshooter'**.

So JSB asked him what he did that was different.

The technician said: **"Well suppose this copier here had an 'intermittent image quality fault,' what would you do?"**

So JSB looked in the handbook, which said: **"Print out 1,000 copies, sort through until you locate the bad ones, then compare the faulty ones against the original."**

The technician said: **"If you print 1,000 copies at five seconds per copy, that's 200 minutes, or three hours. Plus all that wasted paper and ink."**

JSB asked him what he did that was different.

The technician said: **"I walk over to the waste-bin and turn it upside down. I know every copy in there is bad, that's why it was thrown away. Then I compare them against the originals and I've got my answer. Saves three hours printing plus a ton of paper and all that ink."**

Ten years later, Steve Jobs would use the thinking JSB developed at PARC to revolutionise the world of computers.

He would start with people and what they wanted, instead of starting with technology and what it could do.

Steve Jobs understood the whole point is to give people what they want and need.

EQUAL DOESN'T MEAN THE SAME

Aimee Scott is 21, she teaches eighth grade (seven-year-olds) in Utah.

The kids are new to school and some of them have special needs, so Aimee has something she does with them before she starts lessons.

She asks the class if anyone has ever fallen over and scraped their elbow.

Obviously all the kids have, so they hold their hands up.

She asks one of them to come up to the front and tell the story.

Then she gives them a band-aid for their elbow.

Everyone can see this is a kind gesture and makes sense.

Then she asks if anyone has ever had a stomach ache.

Again, everyone holds their hands up.

She asks one of them to come to the front of class and tell the story.

Then she gives them a band-aid for their elbow, as well.

Everyone doesn't quite get it, how does a band-aid help a stomach ache?

Then she asks if anyone has ever had a cold and sneezing.

Again, everyone holds their hand up.

She asks one of them to come to the front and tell the story.

Then she also gives them a band-aid for their elbow.

By now the kids are confused, how can a band-aid help sneezing?

The she asks if anyone has ever had a headache.

Everyone holds their hands up.

She asks them to come to the front of class and tell the story.

Then she gives them a band-aid for their elbow.

By now the kids are really confused, how does a band-aid help a headache?

Eventually she explains to the children that a band-aid isn't right in all cases.

Everyone's got a different problem so they all need a different solution, not everyone needs the same thing.

Aimee says this works with the class because it's simple and obvious, everyone can see it makes sense.

And it helps during lessons because one of the children might have diabetes, and they might need a sugary sweet occasionally.

If she gives them one, and one of the other children says: **"Why can't I have a sweet?"** Aimee can remind them by just saying: **"Remember the band-aid?"**

And the child remembers that not everyone needs the same thing.

It works when one of her children, with autism, needs noise-cancelling headphones and another child wants headphones too, she can just say **"band-aid"** and they remember.

Or when one of her children with ADHD needs a fidget spinner, and another child wants a fidget spinner, too.

Aimee, or one of the children, will just say **"band-aid"** and everyone immediately remembers that it isn't unfair that one person gets something different.

Fair doesn't mean everyone gets the same, fair means everyone gets what they need.

Aimee really understands communication: make it simple, make it catchy, make it fun.

Make it something they can easily understand and want to remember.

In our terms, make it a message people want to repeat long after the ad is finished.

Instead of something so boring they forget it before the packshot's faded.

If it doesn't live outside of the media we've paid for, it's wasted money.

Going viral shouldn't be something special, it should be the standard requirement.

Our message should live in the mind of the consumer, not die on the screen.

Whether we personally like the communication or not is irrelevant.

Whether the communication works with the target market is everything.

WHEN THE ANSWER ASKS THE QUESTION

Jorge Odon owned a garage in Buenos Aires.

In 2006, one of his mechanics was demonstrating a trick he'd seen on YouTube.

How to extract a cork that was rolling around inside an empty wine bottle.

The other mechanics tried shaking the bottle, spearing the cork, nothing worked.

So he showed them how it was done: twist a plastic bag until it's long and thin, then thread it into the neck of the bottle and blow into the bag so that, as it inflates, it traps the cork against the glass side.

Then slowly pull the bag out, the bag holds the cork and the cork pops out.

For a mechanic like Jorge, this was counter-intuitive, it shouldn't work but it did.

It had to be useful for something more than a party trick.

And it stayed with him, nagging at him, what could it be used for?

Until one night he sat up in bed and he thought of women giving birth.

At the time Jorge didn't know the exact numbers, but he knew there was a problem.

The numbers actually are: 13.7 million women a year suffer birth complications.

5.6 million babies are stillborn, or die soon after – 260,000 women die in childbirth.

In the developed world, for an obstructed labour, the safe answer is a caesarean section.

But in most of the world the only resort is forceps or a suction cup.

Forceps are large, rounded pincers, unchanged for four hundred years.

Wrongly used, they can result in a haemorrhage, crushed skull, or twisted spine.

Jorge got a jar from the kitchen and his daughter's doll and began to experiment.

Eventually he developed a way to insert a polythene bag until it surrounded the baby's head then gently pulled it out.

(The baby didn't need to breathe, it got oxygen via the umbilical cord.)

A friend introduced him to an obstetrician, who was sceptical about listening to a car mechanic but arranged a meeting with the chief obstetrician at Buenos Aires hospital.

He was also sceptical about listening to a car mechanic, but arranged for him to meet the head of the World Health Organisation, who was lecturing in Buenos Aires.

Dr. Merialdi was sceptical about listening to a car mechanic, but agreed to ten minutes.

Ten minutes became two hours, then he arranged research at Des Moines University.

At the World Economic Forum in Davos, Becton Dickinson & Co invested $20 million in producing the design.

Now it's in development and Jorge has already witnessed it deliver 30 healthy babies.

It will sell to the developing world for 25% of the price it sells for in the developed world.

All because Jorge, a mechanic, came up with the solution before the problem.

As Dr. Merialdi said: **"An obstetrician would have tried to improve the forceps or the vacuum extractor, but obstructed labour needed a mechanic. And ten years ago this would not have been possible, without YouTube, he would not have seen the video."**

Sometimes the answer comes before the question.

John Webster's office always had a wall full of great techniques that he knew he was going to use one day, and he always did.

Charles Saatchi would say to creatives: **"Don't throw that away"** when he rejected something, knowing it would be useful later.

Ron Collins had a collection of postcards and books he knew he would use one day.

At GGT, we had a bookcase full of video techniques waiting for anyone to use if they fitted an idea.

We had a motto I learned from working with John Webster: **"The best time to look for an idea is before you need it."**

Or, as Helmut Krone said: **"Sometimes you make the revolution, then you decide what it's for."**

YOU SNOOZE, YOU LOSE

There are 3.24 million cashpoint machines (ATMs) in use worldwide.

But the invention of the cashpoint is a typically British bodge story.

It didn't have teams of electronic engineers working in research and development labs.

It had one eccentric Scotsman named John Shepherd-Barron.

In the 1950s he wanted some cash out of the bank, but they shut at 3 pm in those days.

So he couldn't get his own money out of his own bank account.

This annoyed him and, in his bath, a thought struck him, why not get machines to dispense cash the way machines dispensed chocolate bars?

He worked on the idea and eventually persuaded Barclays bank.

He used cheque-like paper tokens impregnated with radioactive Carbon-14 (it wasn't dangerous, you'd have to eat 136,000 cheques to have any ill effects).

Shepherd-Barron wanted a six-figure PIN, but his wife could only remember four numbers, which is why we have a four-figure PIN.

He thought withdrawals should be limited to £10, which he felt was **"Quite sufficient for a wild weekend."**

In 1967 it was launched at Barclays' Enfield branch, the first withdrawal was made by Reg Varney (who played a bus driver in the TV sitcom **'On the Buses'.)**

Later, John Shepherd-Barron received an OBE for his invention.

Which really infuriated another Scotsman, James Goodfellow, who says he was the real inventor of the ATM.

A year before Shepherd-Barron unveiled his cashpoint machine, Goodfellow had officially patented his.

The banks were worried that the unions were going to stop bank staff working Saturday mornings, which was the only time working people could access their cash.

So Goodfellow had to get 2,000 ATMs available for one million bank customers.

And Goodfellow's version had the plastic card we use today, not a radioactive cheque.

He was angry about not getting the credit because: **"The race to get it on the street was not as important. Getting it right was the answer, not getting it first."**

But, as we know, in the public's mind that isn't true.

In Ries and Trout's book, *Positioning*, they say it's binary, the public divide any market into two: number one and everybody else.

The public don't study every single market in fine detail.

That's why everyone remembers Isaac Newton as the inventor of calculus, despite the fact that it's Leibniz's version we use today.

That's why everyone remembers Picasso as the inventor of Cubism, not Braque.

That's why everyone remembers Edison as the inventor of the lightbulb, not Joseph Swan.

That's why everyone remembers Marconi as the inventor of radio, not Nikola Tesla.

That's why everyone remembers Steve Jobs as the inventor of the computer mouse, the scroll-down menu, and desktop publishing.

Despite the fact that he admits taking all those ideas from the Palo Alto Research Center.

So, in our terms, Goodfellow got it exactly wrong.

If he wanted the credit for inventing the ATM machine, the object was to stake a claim in the public's consciousness.

Differentiation is crucial, without that we're just part of the mass.

But differentiation will give us clarity and identity in one of the thousands of categories fighting for attention in their daily lives.

Amanda Walsh used to tell me the retail mantra was: **"One is wonderful. Two is tolerable. Three is threatened. Four is forgotten."**

WHO SAYS I HAVE TO DO IT THAT WAY?

After the floods last June, our wooden conservatory was rotted.

It was two storeys tall with a lead roof that weighed about two tons.

I asked a surveyor to have a look. He said it would all have to be replaced.

I said: **"All except the roof, there's nothing wrong with the roof."**

He said: **"No, the roof as well. While you're replacing all that two-storey wood framing there's nothing to support the roof, and that's at least two tons of lead.**

So instead of trying to prop it all up, it'd be better to pull the lot down and start again."

He said it would take at least three weeks and cost a fortune, with the entire back of the house being open all that time.

And he quoted me a figure for the job that nearly made me fall over.

As a recommendation is always the best way to go, I asked a friend.

He said he knew a really good builder, so I asked them to give me a quote.

The builder came and looked at the job and quoted half what the surveyor had.

I asked him what he thought about taking the roof down.

He said: **"No, the roof's in good nick, no need to touch that."**

I asked about the whole back of the house being opened for three weeks.

He said: **"No it won't. There are five large panels in the conservatory, so we replace one panel at a time – takes about one day per panel to replace it.**

So the roof is always supported by the other panels and the back of your house is never left open. Should take about a week to do the whole job."

The surveyor said that was the wrong way to do it; the builder said it wasn't.

The surveyor said: **"Don't tell me, I've been doing this for twenty years."**

The builder said: **"Well maybe you've been doing it wrong for twenty years."**

I love that answer.

We gave the builder the job. He turned up at 7.30am the next day. I said: **"Do you start work today?"**

He said: **"No, today is just for prep-work, covering everything with dustsheets and rubber mats, putting wooden boxes round everything. So tomorrow we can get stuck straight in."**

And they did. Four builders turned up and began removing the old conservatory, replacing one panel at a time at a rate of one day per panel.

As one panel came out, a new one went straight in. There was never any strain on the roof, so there was no need to replace it.

Cathy made them tea and biscuits at regular intervals, and they worked like a well-drilled team, it was a pleasure to watch.

But what I loved best was the answer to the surveyor's **"I've been doing it for years."**

The builder's response was: **"Well, maybe you've been doing it wrong for years."**

I think that's a great lesson in creativity.

After the surveyor had gone, the builder said to me: **"You gotta be able to think outside the box, ain't ya? Surveyors don't actually get their hands dirty, they've never actually done the job. They just quote in big numbers whatever's easiest for them."**

And I thought, I love it, I'm learning creativity from a builder.

Then I thought, people in advertising and marketing are like that surveyor – we just give you the same old answers that we, and everyone else, have learned.

That's how they got their surveyor's qualifications without ever thinking differently.

That's because they learned from people who never thought differently.

Consequently, unlike that builder, they can't think for themselves.

Then I thought: as a client, who would I rather employ, the surveyor or the builder?

Then I thought: who would I rather be like, the surveyor or the builder?

PHONING IT IN

In 1889, Almon Strowger was an undertaker in Kansas City, Missouri.

In his spare time he liked to invent things.

Which was just as well because he had lots of spare time, business was terrible.

He couldn't work out why, there was only one other undertaker in town.

But everyone used the other undertaker and no one used Almon Strowger.

One day he found a friend of his had used the other undertaker to bury a deceased relative.

He asked the friend why he didn't come to him.

The friend said he tried to call on the phone, but the woman who ran the phone exchange said his number was busy.

She redirected him to the other undertaker instead.

Strowger didn't understand it, his phone was never busy, so he got another friend to call the exchange and ask for his number.

Even though his phone wasn't busy, the woman at the exchange said it was, and redirected him to the other undertaker.

That's when Strowger found out that the woman who ran the telephone exchange was the other undertaker's wife.

She'd been redirecting all his calls to the other undertaker for ages.

Because that's how the early telephones worked, they didn't have dials.

When you wanted to make a call, you picked up the phone and it connected you to a telephonist at the exchange.

You told her who you wanted and she connected you.

This particular telephonist had simply been redirecting all Strowger's calls to her husband.

That's when the inventor in Almon Strowger got angry.

To get even, he would invent something that would put that woman out of a job.

An automatic telephone exchange wouldn't do what she'd been doing.

It would have to put the caller through to whoever they wanted.

And, in the days before transistors and technology, he invented a mechanical switching system.

He built the prototype from pins and a cardboard hat box.

Because it was mechanical, the parts had to physically move, which meant slowing everything down.

That's why he invented the rotary dial on the telephone.

Because everything had to be mechanical, ten was the greatest number of connections he could fit on a rotor, so he simply had each extension connected to another rotor: 10 x 10 = 100 possible connections.

In 1891, he was granted a patent, and in 1892 the first-ever automatic exchange was installed in La Porte, Indiana.

The town had 75 telephones, and his automatic exchange could handle 99.

As we know, Strowger's exchange did in fact put the other undertaker's wife, and every other telephonist, out of work.

He even referenced her in the advertising for his new automatic exchange: **"Girl-less. Cuss-less. Out-of-order-less. Wait-less."**

Strowger's patent was eventually sold to Bell Systems in 1916 and allowed them to dominate the market.

In time, Bell Systems became the Bell Telephone Company, and eventually AT&T.

By the 1980s, they were worth $150 billion and employed a million people.

The main learning from Almon Strowger is, don't confront the problem head on.

The more you oppose a problem, the stronger it gets, so bypass the problem.

Think upstream of it and you bypass it, and it disappears.

INTELLIGENCE ALONE ISN'T CREATIVE

Today, the word 'creativity' usually refers to the latest electronic innovation.

But technology and innovation aren't the same as creativity.

This was Amy Smith's worry.

She lectured in mechanical engineering at Massachusetts Institute of Technology (MIT).

In 2002 she opened the D-Lab: standing for 'Development through Discovery, Design, and Dissemination'.

The main course was called Creative Capacity Building and, for her, 'creative' meant practical solutions to global poverty challenges.

Creativity *had* to be practical.

The course ran a workshop headed **"Make what you couldn't make when you walked in"**.

One of her students was Bernard Kiwia, a young man from Tanzania.

What he learned at MIT was more revolutionary than mere electronic innovation.

The creativity he took back to Tanzania was how to transform a village with no electricity.

If no one in the village had electricity, where could he start?

Well the one thing everyone did have was a bicycle.

So first he turned his bicycle into a charger for his mobile phone.

Then he made a pedal-powered water pump for his bicycle to run.

Then a pedal-powered washing machine.

Then he made a solar-powered water heater.

Soon the locals wanted this creative technology, so Bernard copied MIT's D-Lab.

He began teaching locals to solve problems with *practical* creativity.

So far, Frank Mollel has created the 'Fert cart' from a wheelbarrow.

It spreads manure and fertiliser much faster and more evenly than can be done by hand.

He sells or rents them, and the proceeds mean he can send his children to school.

Jesse Oljange was able to design and manufacture a home-made avocado oil-press.

So instead of letting excess fruit rot on the ground it can be collected and turned into oil to be stored or sold.

Magreth Omary was able to make a soap cutting machine which means she now runs a small factory employing local women.

There's also a home-made maize-sheller which can process 100kg of maize per hour.

Also a machine for turning avocado seeds into powder, for making herbal teas.

Wood is in short supply, so they are making beehives from waste plastic.

A mechanical fruit juicer means fallen fruit doesn't go to waste, it's sold as juice instead.

A plough and planter device can do both jobs simultaneously, cultivating twice the land.

Bernard Kiwia estimates around 800 local inventors have benefitted so far.

Using creativity to invent products, sell them and make money for food and education.

So MIT's D-Lab is having a real effect in the world by Developing *real* creativity where it can make a *real* difference.

That is why Edward de Bono stressed practicality:

"An idea that can be developed and put into action is many times more important than an idea that exists only as an idea."

In the West, and particularly in advertising and marketing, we tend to value theoretical thinking highly.

This has the appearance of knowledge but often has no practical value.

That's why de Bono insisted practicality is a measure of creativity.

Creativity has to have a purpose.

"Many highly intelligent people are poor thinkers.

Many people of average intelligence are skilled thinkers.

The power of the car is separate from the way the car is driven."

PART 2

WHEN ORDINARY IS EXTRAORDINARY

ADVERTISING FOR REAL PEOPLE

On his radio show, Chris Evans was discussing Piers Morgan being fired.

The news presenter, Rachel Horne, said she'd had to explain it to her young sons at dinner the previous night.

Chris asked why they were interested in Piers Morgan.

Rachel said: **"They said 'he's a news presenter and you're a news presenter Mummy, does that mean you could get fired?'**

So she said: **'No, there are two types of news presenters and we're both different.'"**

The little boys asked what the difference was.

She said: **"Well some presenters just give you the facts, while other presenters give you their opinion."**

The little boys asked what she meant.

So she said: **"Well tonight you're having pasta bake for dinner. Now the way I would report on that is to say that it's made from wheat and cheese, and Quorn because it's vegetarian. Then I might ask you what you each think of it."**

Her first son said he liked it, it tasted really good.

Her second son said he liked it because he could eat it with his spoon.

She said: **"Okay, so I'd sum up by saying that all the people we interviewed were happy with their pasta bake and seemed willing to have it for dinner again."**

The boys nodded along, but they wanted to know what Piers Morgan would do.

She said: **"Okay, he'd say 'We've got some vegetarian rubbish here today, I don't know what's wrong with a decent piece of meat but there you go, what do these people think?'"**

Her first son said: **"Well as I said, I like it because..."**

She interrupted: **"Absolute rubbish, we don't want any of that hippie nonsense. You there – what do you think?"**

Her second son said: **"Well I like it, too because..."**

She interrupted again: **"Total nonsense, the country's gone mad, we all need a decent meal made with real meat to sort us out."**

Then she said to her boys: **"That's the two sort of news presenters. I give you the facts while Piers Morgan just gives you his opinion.**

So you can see we're quite different, that's why you don't have to worry about me getting fired like Piers."

And her sons were reassured and went back to eating their pasta bake.

I like several things she did there.

First, I like the way she took something in front of them to use as a demonstration: the pasta bake that they were all eating.

This made it real and accessible, not theoretical, not abstract.

Second, I like the way she made it a simple presentation of the two kinds of news, not saying which was better, just demonstrating the difference.

Third, I like the way she made the boys answer the questions themselves, getting them involved instead of just having to sit there and listen.

Fourth, I like the simple binary summary, not a complicated list of all the possible subtle differences.

I think that's a great demonstration of what advertising should be doing.

Taking a complicated situation, simplifying it, clarifying it, demonstrating it, involving our audience.

All possible nuances can be added once the structure of the choice is clear.

Simple understanding stays with people much longer than a lecture.

SIMPLE, TIMELESS TRUTHS

Cathy and I once took the kids on a safari holiday in South Africa.

While we were walking through the bush, I asked the ranger something that had always puzzled me: what was a rogue elephant?

I'd seen films of them going crazy and destroying everything: was it an elephant in pain from a broken tusk or a thorn in its foot?

The ranger laughed and said no, that was just a cartoon myth.

A real rogue elephant meant that all the older males in the herd had died off, or been killed off by poachers.

So there was nothing to stop the young males going wild, their testosterone was beginning to kick in and they'd rampage around doing whatever they felt like.

With all the older males gone, there was no one to stop them going crazy.

In that case, what the rangers did was to bring in a couple of older males from another herd.

The older males would exert their authority pretty firmly, the younger males quickly got back in line and peace and order was restored.

That's how it works amongst elephants, for years I wondered if there was anything we, as humans, could learn from that.

Then recently I saw a video about Southwood High School in Shreveport, Louisiana.

Apparently this school had a terrible record of violence, it reached crisis point when the police were called 23 times in just three days to arrest students for fighting.

Something had to be done, and Michael LaFitte had an idea what that something was.

He was a parent and he organised 40 of the other fathers into a group called 'Dads on Duty'.

They had t-shirts printed and would take it in turns to make sure there were dads in attendance to greet the students every morning, then throughout the day walk around the school exchanging smiles, banter, and just being a presence.

But all the while these are still dads, and they're BIG guys, so the message is there but it's unsaid: tough love and gentle ribbing.

Since the dads appeared there hasn't been a single incident of fighting or violence.

One male student said, **"We felt safer, we stopped fighting and started going to class."**

One female student said, **"The school has been happy, and you can feel it."**

Another girl talked about the dad 'stare' that could stop students in their tracks.

Michael LaFitte said, **"Not everyone has a father figure or a male, period, in their life. So just to be here makes a big difference."**

As LaFitte implies, a lot of those kids are from single-parent families, with no male role model at home to keep them in line.

So what he's organised is the equivalent of recognising the rogue males and bringing in some older males from another herd to restore order.

And sure enough, the presence of the older males has had just that effect, which means everyone is more structured and settled.

So there *was* something we could learn from the elephants after all.

For me, it's one of Bill Bernbach's **"Simple, timeless, truths"**.

The young males' bodies grow faster than their minds, they are men on the outside but still children on the inside.

So they are naughty and misbehave, like a child, but with a man's body and strength.

But bringing in an older male has the effect of a parent on a child's mind, they defer to parental authority and calmness and order is restored.

This doesn't mean things can't ever change, but change has to be managed.

Change should be improvement, not just destruction.

Mark Zuckerberg's twin maxims, **"Young people are just smarter"** and **"Move fast and break things"** are the rogue elephant's approach to change.

USE YOUR DISADVANTAGE

Jerry Della Femina was a top creative in New York at a time when New York's creatives were the best in the world.

In those days, nearly all great creatives came from the rough part of Brooklyn.

They were Jewish and Italian kids, street-smart and always thinking competitively.

Before them the business was full of posh, white university graduates.

You would have thought the rich, spoilt kids would have had an advantage, but it was the other way round.

The rich kids had grown up protected and polished, but their education was academic.

The kids from Brooklyn didn't have an academic education, their education had taught them street smarts.

They didn't learn history, and Latin, and calculus, and politics, and economics.

They learned how *real* life works.

They had to learn to think from the minute they woke up until they went to bed.

So they were always looking for an angle, a different way to come at things.

Della Femina puts it like this:

"Let me point out the lesson in analytics you learn by going to the track for the last race.

They let you in free for the last race and the track is filled with people who have lost all day long and are betting longshots in the last race to try to get even.

Meanwhile, you bet the horse who was going to be the favourite (and he has a 60% chance of winning), on the last race, since

everyone is betting on the long shots, the favourite goes off at the best odds, 3 to 1 instead of even money."

That's a very creative (unexpected) use of logic.

Most people judge their bet by the odds they see on the board before the race.

He's suggesting you don't do that.

The odds are determined by the amount of money going down.

Longshots pay better odds, so the people trying to get even will be putting their money on the longshots.

The favourite would normally get low odds just because it's the favourite.

So don't bet the favourites in the earlier races when the odds will be evens or lower.

Wait until the last race when the odds will be artificially inflated to 3 to 1.

This is understanding human nature (how people bet) plus how statistics work (odds betting) and there's more to betting than just picking a horse.

That's not a class they teach posh kids at posh schools, that's street smarts.

Another name for it is entrepreneurialism, another name is creativity.

Where I grew up the most common mantra was 'Use your loaf' (loaf of bread = head).

You'd hear it every time you did something without thinking, my dad or one of my mates would shake their head and say "Use your loaf."

That phrase sticks in your head and governs your behaviour, it forces you to think.

I was talking to a group of black kids from Lewisham who wanted to get into advertising.

They were wearing suits and taking elocution lessons.

I told them the worst thing they could do was to try to copy the middle-class kids they saw already in advertising.

All you can ever be is a second-best version of whatever you're trying to copy.

But they had a massive advantage, growing up working class in a poor part of town; they had street smarts.

The middle-class kids didn't have that.

So don't play the game their way, change the game.

Concentrate on using street smarts, it means you won't rest on your laurels like they will, so you'll always be thinking several steps ahead of them.

We've already got more than enough conventional thinkers, the real opportunity is for people who don't think like everyone else.

Make the most of your advantage: use your disadvantage.

USE YOUR LOAF

When I was a teenager, I had a mate called John Nye, who serviced the vending machines that dispensed chocolate bars and coffee at Ford.

John told me what fascinated him was the effort some blokes would go to, to cheat.

The machines only took 10p pieces and were calibrated to measure the coins precisely and to weigh them exactly.

Any coins that didn't match the size and weight were rejected.

And yet there were always some metal discs amongst the change in the machines.

That meant some people were spending ages to make perfect copies of those 10p coins.

The measurements were so exact it took a good few hours' work to machine the fake coins to such tight tolerances.

Now the average wage at Ford in those days was £20 a week, and most workers were on piece-work: the more work they did, the more money they earned.

So four hours work, that's half a day, was costing that worker £2 in wages – that's £2 in order to save 10p.

On what planet does that make sense?

But that's how some people are, they can't think beyond the immediately obvious.

They can only see that they've saved 10p, not that it cost them £2 to do it.

I was brought up with the constant mantra: **"Use your loaf."**

When that is drummed into you, you question everything.

Consequently, I didn't see the cost in terms of money, but in terms of time.

The cost of a chocolate bar from that vending machine is four hours if you make a forged coin, or five minutes if you pay with money you earned.

It seemed to me that putting all that work into saving 10p was small-time thinking.

But they couldn't think further than saving 10p, they couldn't work out the real cost.

The real cost isn't money, the real cost is opportunity.

If it takes four hours to save 10p, what else could you be doing with that time and how much more would that be worth?

It reminds me of the way many people in our business think small instead of big.

When I came into advertising, nearly all posters were 16-sheet, it took Mike Yershon at CDP to invent 48-sheets by putting three 16-sheets together.

At BMP, I used to ask our media guys why we did 16s instead of 48s, and they told me we got more exposure that way.

But getting three times as many crosses on the media chart doesn't mean three times as much exposure in the real world.

Everyone would stop and look at CDP's 48-sheets, they dominated the entire street, whereas our 16-sheets just disappeared amongst all the others.

The same was true of press-ads; most agencies would do quarter-page ads because they got more of them.

David Puttnam tells how CDP was the first to put all of its media money into a double page spread, which dominated the entire publication while all those quarter pages were invisible.

Frank Lowe insisted CDP do 60-second TV ads, while the rest of us were forced to do 15-second ads, because we got more spots.

CDP did fewer ads, but their ads dominated the medium, whereas we ran lots more ads but were much less visible.

We were doing the same as those guys that spent lots of time making fake coins.

We were thinking small because it seemed obvious.

Which is why CDP was voted the best UK agency of the entire twentieth century.

They were always thinking bigger, always thinking upstream, always using their loaf.

WORDS GO VIRAL

In 1862, the Homestead Act was passed in the US, giving settlers 160 acres of land each.

The idea was to get the population to spread west into the vast open plains.

The settlers wanted their 160 acres fenced in, so they could grow crops without having them trampled or eaten.

The distances were vast, and ordinary wire fences would just get knocked over.

So in 1874, Joseph Glidden patented a process for mass-producing barbed wire.

Pretty soon he was selling over three million pounds of it a year to the settlers.

With the distances between the farms so vast, the settlers rarely ever saw another soul.

True, the phone had been invented, but nobody could afford one.

Even if they could it wouldn't matter, it didn't make sense for the phone companies to run cables over all that distance for so few users.

Which is when the farmers found a use for all those miles and miles of barbed wire.

They hooked up old wooden box telephones to it and used it as phone cable.

Of course it was crude, you couldn't just dial a number, but that didn't matter.

It was a way for everyone to connect to each other, everyone could listen in all-at-once or separately.

If you were lonely, you just joined in with whoever was on it.

If you needed help urgently, you didn't have to travel hours into town, you just asked whoever was closest to pass the message on.

If you wanted the news but couldn't afford a radio, you listened in at a certain time every day when someone would read the newspaper over it.

At other times, people who could play the banjo or fiddle would link up and have a rough-and-ready sing-song.

You might have a particular signal for certain friends, three long or three short rings, that would signal who you wanted to pick up and that it was private.

It might sound annoying to us, the lack of privacy, but remember these people had never had a phone, or radio, or TV, or any way to contact the outside world.

But they found a way to turn a lifeless object like barbed wire into a community, and it continued well into the 1950s.

Because people wanted to talk, and they found a way to make it happen.

A bunch of experts sitting in an office didn't say, "I've got an idea, let's make barbed wire that can double up as a telephone line."

The hardware wasn't made because experts envisioned its communication possibilities.

Ordinary people wanted to share language, so they found a way to make it happen.

That's what we should remember if we want our work to go viral.

The main thing people want to share is language.

That's why purely visual, international award-winning ads don't go viral.

At international awards, everyone on the jury speaks a different language.

So the ads with the best chance of winning will be purely visual.

But visuals don't go viral, because people can't repeat visuals like language.

Words are what get passed on, so words are what go viral.

It's crucial for us to remember that if we want our work to go viral.

People adapted barbed wire as a means of using words.

Right now what I'm using are words, not pictures.

Of course visuals are important, but what gets repeated are words not pictures.

That's how people communicate.

We are in the communications business.

If we don't start with what works, we are in the wrong business.

COME OFF BROADCAST, GO ON RECEIVE

In Vietnam, US troops were issued with the most modern rifle ever: the M16.

It was a good design but, by the time the procurement people had finished, it wasn't.

They interfered and made it on the cheap, so the parts got bent and clogged and jammed.

But, as typical paper-pushers, they thought the way to fix it was to pretend.

So they sent the M16 out to all fighting troops, telling them this was the best weapon ever.

And the troops believed it, they didn't know it was prone to jamming at the slightest clog, the slightest damp, the slightest bump.

None of which is ideal for a weapon whose primary function was fighting in the muddy, humid jungle.

But the troops bought the line about it being a wonder weapon, and many of them thought it cleaned itself.

So, many troops were found dead next to their M16s, which were jammed and clogged.

They needed to quickly correct the damage done by issuing a bad weapon and pretending it was a good one.

What was needed was a 32-page manual detailing all the necessary procedures each soldier needed to perform to maintain it.

But how do you get young boys, who'd just come over from the States, to learn the lengthy process of cleaning and caring for a complicated piece of equipment?

Teenagers wouldn't read army pamphlets, they'd never study official publications that were as boring as schoolbooks.

Luckily, this was where someone with a brain got involved.

They knew that all teenage boys cared about was comics, girls, and baseball.

They spent all their time reading comics, and they had pinups on their walls: *Playboy* gatefolds, and baseball stars.

So, in 1968, they got the best comic book artist in America, Will Eisner, to put together a maintenance manual comprising those elements.

It was in the form of a comic book, the spokesperson throughout was a curvy Anne Margaret lookalike dressed in fatigues, who spoke in speech bubbles.

A lot of it was in cheeky *double entendre*, the sort of language to make young men laugh and remember.

Lines like: TREAT YOUR RIFLE LIKE A LADY, and SWEET 16 AND NEVER MISSED, and HOW TO STRIP YOUR BABY, and TRY OGLING THESE MAGAZINE PINUPS (for maintenance of the ammunition magazine).

And they'd switch into baseball language: WHEN THE BASES ARE LOADED EVERY HIT COUNTS, and LAID A BUNT LATELY, and SOME GUYS SPOIL A PLAY BY REACHING OUT FOR BALLS NOT MEANT FOR 'EM – BUMPED HEADS AND LOST GAMES RESULT.

The curvy female spokesperson would occasionally lapse into the sort of jargon that was common amongst soldiers in Vietnam: FOR ALL YOU M16 ZAPSTERS HERE ARE SOME NUMBAH ONE SUGGESTIONS TO KEEP YOU ON THE GO-GO.

The cover of the comic wasn't a formal War Department document either.

The headline on the booklet said: HEY SARGE, GET THIS COPY TO THE MAN WITH THE RIFLE.

It showed a sergeant and a GI, bullets flying all around them, the sergeant saying: **"Do me a favor, do a quick 'before-operations' check on your rifle BEFORE we counter-attack."**

The great thing was because it was a comic no one threw it away.

Because it was a comic they read it, again and again.

Because they read it, they remembered it.

Because they remembered it, it saved lives.

The incidence of dead soldiers with clogged and broken rifles declined.

Which is why we must talk to the audience in the language they prefer, NOT in the language we prefer.

THE CLARITY OF DESPERATION

Strange that the Americans who pride themselves most on being patriotic are anti-vaxxers.

Many years ago George Washington, perhaps the greatest patriot of all, decided to make vaccinations mandatory.

Historians agree that without those vaccinations, America could have lost the war and would not now be a country but a British colony.

What happened was, in 1776, smallpox was killing a huge chunk of Washington's Continental Army and spreading fast.

It didn't affect the British troops because most had survived smallpox when they were young, so they were immune.

But at one point, 90% of the deaths among American Continental regulars were caused by disease, not by British troops.

So Washington had to make a decision, he had three choices:

1. Wait for herd immunity: let nature take its course and let many die.

2. Quarantine: lock the troops away so they couldn't fight.

3. Inoculation: risk an experimental procedure that might work.

This is pretty much what we'd call a no-brainer, the first two are definitely losing strategies, the third was a gamble but at least it was a chance.

It was called 'variolation' and involved making a cut into the arm and inserting a thread into the incision that had been dipped in the pus from an infected person.

The Continental Congress had banned variolation in 1776.

But Washington, owing to the clarity of desperation, overrode them.

Of course this form of treatment was crude and people died, but 5% died instead of 30%.

In 1777, he wrote to John Hancock: **"The small pox has made such Head in every Quarter that I find it impossible to keep it from spreading thro' the whole Army in the natural way. I have therefore determined, not only to innoculate all the Troops now here, that have not had it, but shall order Docr Shippen to innoculate the Recruits as fast as they come into Philadelphia."**

And so, instead of having a dying army, Washington won the war and a country.

Of course, he didn't discover the actual vaccine for smallpox, that was Edward Jenner in England 20 years later, in 1796.

Jenner noticed milkmaids, who had contracted cowpox, were immune to smallpox.

He had heard of variolation and wondered if this might be better.

So he took some pus from a sore on an infected milkmaid's hand and scratched it into the arm of his gardener's son.

Then he exposed the boy to smallpox victims, and the boy remained uninfected.

In 1801, Jenner published his paper: **'On the Origin of Vaccine Inoculation'**.

By the twentieth century, the entire planet was inoculated, and nobody has died of smallpox since 1978.

In 1980 the WHO declared the world free of smallpox.

But the interesting part for us is Washington's dilemma.

If he inoculated his army, then 5% would die.

But if he did nothing, then 30% of his men would die and he would lose the war.

There was NO situation in which no one dies, much as he would have preferred it.

While we are sitting around discussing a perfect solution that does not exist, we do nothing which means we lose control of the situation.

This was the real-life version of **'The Trolley Problem'**, the philosophical thought experiment: If you do nothing, four men die, if you pull a lever one man dies, what do you do?

Most of us freeze because of the paralysis caused by evading responsibility.

Most of us would rather suffer the consequences of inaction.

What saved George Washington was the **'clarity of desperation'**.

We should learn from that.

HOW TO BE HUMAN

I've never been a fan of the Royal Family.

But then I heard an episode of the radio show Desert Island Discs that gave me pause for thought.

The guest was a top London surgeon, David Nott.

He regularly took time off from his practice to work in war zones: Darfur, Sierra Leone, Congo, Syria.

He talked about the gunfire, the bombs, the missile attacks, the lack of equipment, the lack of blood for transfusions.

He talked about his first time in Sarajevo, when the lights went off in the middle of an operation, leaving everything pitch black.

When the lights came back on he was alone. All the operating staff had just disappeared, leaving him to do the operation alone.

He talked about Syria in 2013, when he was operating on the open chest of an ISIS fighter.

Six men entered and trained their AK47s on him while he worked.

He operated for half an hour with legs like jelly.

He talked about Gaza in 2014, when he was operating on a little girl whose bowels, stomach, bladder, and spleen were hanging out from shrapnel wounds.

Suddenly everyone was told to leave because the hospital would be blown up in five minutes.

He thought, **"If I leave, the little girl dies."**

And he thought, since he didn't have a family to worry about, he would risk it, stay and finish the operation.

Luckily, the bomb didn't explode and he saved the little girl's life.

But he didn't realise, all of this had given him PTSD, and ten days after all this he was at Buckingham Palace sitting next to the Queen for lunch.

The contrast was too great, too sudden. He froze – he couldn't speak.

And this is where, he said, the Queen showed great human insight. She asked the butler to bring the corgis in, then she asked for some biscuits.

Then she asked David Nott if he'd like to help her feed the corgis.

And he said that interacting with animals, stroking them and feeding them, was the perfect response to his PTSD.

He calmed down and was able to sit with the Queen, quietly chatting for half an hour.

He says it showed real human understanding.

The very smallness of the gesture allowed him to reconnect with reality, whereas the overpowering opulence of the palace had completely alienated him.

This was a case of less is more, and it's something we all need to learn.

I've recently seen two short pieces of film that resonated more than any expensive Cannes award winners.

One was during the early days of the Covid-19 pandemic.

A teacher wanted to demonstrate to her class of small children why washing their hands was important.

She had a saucer of water and she sprinkled black pepper into it. The pepper represented germs.

She put her finger into the water and pulled it out – the children could see some pepper was stuck to it.

Then she washed the finger in soap and put it back into the saucer.

All the pepper was immediately repelled and rushed to the other side of the saucer.

The children gasped as the finger came out without a speck on it.

That simple demonstration was more effective than any amount of government propaganda.

The second short film I saw was on TikTok. It had no spoken words, just subtitles:

Two lighters are held up, each subtitled: A HUMAN BEING.

One lighter is dropped into a glass, s/t: WHAT YOU DON'T SEE.

Water is added to the glass, s/t: CHILDHOOD TRAUMA.

More water is added, s/t: ABUSE.

More water added, s/t: INSECURITY.

More water, s/t: LONELINESS.

The wet lighter is taken out of the glass. It can't light, s/t: LIFE IS HARD. WE CAN LOSE OUR SPARK.

The dry lighter enters and lights the damp lighter, s/t: SOMETIMES WE NEED HELP.

The damp lighter is now fully alight, s/t: YOU DON'T KNOW THEIR STORY

Then the end title: HELP SOMEONE TODAY @mindbodysouluk.

And those two powerful little demonstrations probably cost less to make than the catering budget on a single Cannes award winner.

Just like the Queen's gesture to the doctor: small and human beats big and boastful.

WE DON'T CONTROL THE CONVERSATION

We like to think we control the conversation, but that isn't how it works in the real world.

For instance, in 1973, there was a run on the Toyokawa Shinkin bank: 2 billion yen was withdrawn in a matter of days because of a rumour of bankruptcy.

The police investigated to see if a crime had been committed.

They traced the rumour back to three schoolgirls on a train.

On 8 December the girls were discussing where they'd be working after graduation, one said she had a job at the Toyokawa Shinkin bank.

The other two, teasing her about bank robberies, said it sounded dangerous.

Later, the girl asked her mother if the Toyokawa Shinkin bank was dangerous.

Her mother misunderstood and asked a relative, who worked at a beauty salon, if she'd heard if the Toyokawa Shinkin bank was in danger.

On 10 December, the relative asked the ladies who came into her beauty salon if they'd heard about the danger of the bank going bust.

One of them owned a dry-cleaner, she asked her customers if they heard the rumours.

Now confirmation bias began to kick in, people heard the rumour back from people who had also heard the rumour, which proved it must have some foundation.

On 13 December the dry-cleaner overheard a customer on the phone withdrawing 1.2 million yen from the bank (for a business expense).

She assumed he was withdrawing his savings, so she withdrew her own 1.8 million yen.

She warned friends who warned friends, and 59 depositors withdrew 50 million yen.

A taxi driver said his passengers escalated from: 2.15 pm **"The bank might be in danger"**; to 2.30 pm **"The bank IS in danger"**; to 4.30 pm **"The bank is going bankrupt"**; to 6.00 pm **"The bank will not open tomorrow."**

A policeman was sent to control the crowd but confirmation bias just proved his presence was further proof of the crisis.

On 14 December, the bank announced they'd pay all withdrawals, but they'd round them down to make repayments faster.

Confirmation bias interpreted this as proof that the bank couldn't even pay interest.

On 15 December Toyokawa Shinkin bank held a press conference displaying a pile of money, one metre high and five metres wide, in the vault.

The national TV station, NHK, denied the rumour, as did newspapers: *Asahi Shimbun*, *Yomiuri Shimbun*, and *Mainichi Shimbun*, plus the Bank of Japan, the Shinkin Central Bank, and the National Association of Shinkin Banks all had to publicly deny the rumour.

The Japanese financial authorities had to officially deny what began as a joke between three schoolgirls on a train.

What is the learning for us in this?

The learning is negativity bias: bad news is more credible and spreads faster.

Richard Shotton quotes Hans Rosling on the subject:

"People think the world is more frightening, more violent, and more hopeless – *in short more dramatic* – **than it really is."**

And Shotton's worry is: **"This negativity bias doesn't just affect the public, it affects professionals too, and it's alive and kicking in marketing today. Think about the headlines and opinion pieces in the trade press. Whether it's the death of TV, declining attention spans or the trust crisis, there's an apocalyptic bent**

to them. And, if our perception differs from reality, we'll make suboptimal decisions."

So, next time you hear advertising is dead, or interruption is dead, or TV is dead, remember how rumours spread.

And remember the old Indian expression, **"When a man has been bitten by a snake he is frightened by a coil of rope."**

And remember *bad* news is more dramatic: when we don't control it, it controls us.

SABOTAGING OURSELVES

In 1944, the OSS was the precursor of the CIA.

Like the CIA, the work of the OSS was spying, sabotage, dirty tricks – anything to disrupt the enemy.

With this in mind, they issued a booklet to be distributed to anyone sympathetic inside occupied territory.

This book was called **A Simple Sabotage Field Manual**.

As you'd expect, it was full of suggestions on physical damage, destroying machinery, delaying production, wrecking transport, and so on.

But the really sneaky part was the section on the great harm the average person could do to the enemy's war effort without any risk of being detected at all.

Sabotage so insidious that it would never be noticed, requiring no tools and producing no physical evidence of damage.

The manual explains the surreptitious nature of these particular actions.

"They are based on universal opportunities to make faulty decisions, to adopt a non-cooperative attitude, and induce others to follow suit."

It specified that: **"Middle managers, especially those with white collar jobs should pontificate, flip-flop, and take every decision into committee."**

They should: **"Bring up irrelevant issues as frequently as possible, haggle over precise wording. Hold conferences when there is more important work to be done."**

Specifically, they listed eight actions which could disrupt morale and production.

Insist on doing everything through channels.

Make speeches. Talk as frequently as possible and at great length.

Haggle over precise wording of communications.

Bring up irrelevant issues as frequently as possible.

Refer back to matters already decided upon and attempt to question the advisability of that decision.

Be worried about the propriety of any decision.

Advocate caution and urge fellow conferees to avoid haste that might result in embarrassment or difficulties later on.

Refer all matters to committees.

These are subtle and destructive tactics for sabotaging decision-making processes in all organisations.

But the really clever part is that they'd never be noticed, because they happen all the time.

Check out the list and see if you can't find several items that happen on a daily basis in your company.

People quibbling about precise wording and missing the whole point of the idea.

People constantly calling unnecessary meetings to discuss work that's already been agreed.

People insisting on scrupulously observing process, even though it results in a dull ad.

People urging caution – anything to avoid perceived risk, however trivial.

People desperate to find someone, anyone, who will be offended by an ad.

We all know we are trying to do our jobs surrounded by people like this.

People who will try to make the whole process as dull and suffocating as possible, so the ads end up being soporific at best and invisible at worst.

And the irony is, these people do it all under the belief that they are doing the job.

We are sabotaging ourselves every day, just as sure as if we'd all read the OSS manual.

We honestly believe it's more professional to act like a handbrake, not like an accelerator.

So we take every opportunity to be the anchor the ship is dragging.

We honestly believe the proper way to work is slower, and safer, and duller.

In taking the advice of the OSS, we are sabotaging ourselves.

PART 3

DON'T LOOK WHERE EVERYONE ELSE IS LOOKING

NEW MEDIA ISN'T EVEN NEW

The first advertising class I ever took was in Brooklyn, two creatives from Madison Avenue came to my college to teach us.

The first project they gave us was to advertise ourselves, just that, no brief.

So that's what we worked on all week, we did what we thought was advertising.

We got our visualiser pads, we drew up ideas for posters, print ads, commercials.

Some of us even made up posters and stuck them up in the street near where they worked.

Some of us went to their agencies and handed out badges.

Then, on the evening of the presentation, we all walked in except one girl who was missing.

The two teachers sat at the front with long faces.

They said: **"There isn't going to be a class tonight, the best student here was killed in a car crash.**

We got a letter from the Dean asking us to collect her work.

She was the best one here, if anyone was going to make it, it was her.

Her work was interesting, exciting, fresh, unusual. It isn't fair that she's gone..."

They carried on eulogising her for at least fifteen minutes, then eventually they just sat there quietly, looking at the floor.

At that moment, the girl poked her head round the door, she said: **"Have you finished? Thanks very much, you just did my advertising for me."**

The two teachers were gobsmacked.

They were furious, they said: **"What the fuck…"** and they couldn't get any more words out.

They threw down the letter and stormed out of the room.

The next week they came back, they had calmed down.

They said that was the worst, cruellest, sneakiest, best, most original and creative way they'd ever seen that project handled.

That girl knew that, in America, whenever anyone dies they receive a eulogy where everyone says nothing but nice things about them.

So, with a minimum of effort, she'd got the two teachers to spend the class just saying nice things about her, doing the project for her in fact.

And better than that, those two creatives carried that letter in their wallets and showed it to all their friends up and down Madison Avenue.

By the time she graduated, every ad agency knew her name and she could have got a job anywhere.

All because she didn't take the word **'advertising'** to mean the conventional solutions the way the rest of us did.

Nowadays, everyone thinks it's a revolutionary thought to say that advertising doesn't just mean conventional media.

That's what all the new media gurus mean when they say **"Advertising is dead."**

But their thinking doesn't extend beyond new media, new technology.

Thinking beyond advertising doesn't just mean using whatever new media is around.

New media is just a new form of the same old conventional thinking.

"Here's the brief, we want to see lots of digital."

What's true is what's always been true: real creativity doesn't restrict itself to what everyone else is thinking.

While the whole class was thinking of conventional advertising, that girl was thinking: **"What's beyond that, what won't anyone else even dare think of?**

Given that everything is potentially media, what is there in the entire world that's fresh and original that I could use?

What is there that no one else would even *think* of as media?"

That was my very first lesson in real creative thinking, many years before new media gurus even existed.

NO PROBLEM, NO OPPORTUNITY

About thirty years ago, an 18-year-old was vandalising trains in a rail-yard.

He was spraying big bubble-lettering along the side of a train: "BE ON TIME FOR ONCE".

Now if you're doing it properly, decent spray painting takes quite a while.

In the middle of spraying it, the police turned up.

He ran, but with all his cans of paint he couldn't run fast enough, so he hid under a lorry.

While the police searched the area he just lay there, with oil dripping on him from the lorry.

He thought to himself: **"I can't keep this up, it takes too long. I've either got to pack it in or find a faster way of doing it."**

As he lay there he looked up at the bottom of the lorry.

On the fuel tank was stencilled: FILL TO LINE ONLY – DO NOT OVERFILL.

And he thought: **"They've stencilled that, it looks perfectly even, every letter the same size, all correctly spaced, but all it took was one quick spray with a spray can."**

Then he thought: **"That's what I'm gonna do, switch to stencilling, do all the hard work at home, cutting out the letters and pictures.**

Then when I get to the site, one quick spray and I'm done."

And when he did it, he was so pleased with the result he wanted to sign it.

But it was illegal, he couldn't use his real name, he needed a name like Robin Hood, so he called himself Robin Banks.

His friends naturally shortened his name, and he became known as Banksy.

So right there is how the problem became the opportunity.

And that pretty much sums up Banksy's subsequent career: look for a problem and turn it into an opportunity.

Wherever Banksy wasn't allowed to paint, that's exactly where he would paint.

The stencilling technique, and the witty satirical content, became unique.

Banksy's work stood out from all the crude tagging that everyone else was doing.

His work was fun, enjoyable, people began buying it, celebrities began collecting it.

Instead of removing it, some councils actually protected it and restored it.

His work even sold at auctions.

In 2018, his artwork, Balloon Girl, was sold at Sotheby's for over £1 million, all the major news networks covered it.

But they got an even bigger story when, as the auctioneer's hammer came down, the artwork began to shred itself, from a shredder built into the frame.

As this was the first time an artwork had ever been destroyed while it was being sold, the value of the piece immediately doubled to £2 million.

Again, Banksy finding out what he wasn't allowed to do and turning it into an opportunity.

He's done the same with paintings, sculpture, films, books, exhibitions: doing what you're not allowed to do has become his media, he now owns that whole area.

By turning problems into opportunities.

When he published his book, he thought a quote from the police on the cover would be a funny thing to have.

So he asked them for a quote, naturally they refused.

So Banksy used their reply on the front cover:

THERE'S NO WAY YOU'RE GOING TO GET A QUOTE FROM US TO USE ON YOUR BOOK COVER – Metropolitan Police Spokesperson.

For most people the problem is what stops us.

As soon as there's a problem we run away from it.

But for Banksy, the problem is where he starts: the problem is the opportunity.

That's why the most creative people behave like an *enfant terrible*.

They look for problems, or they create problems, because that's where the fun is.

YOU DON'T WIN JUST BY GOING FASTER

In 1953, it was a foregone conclusion that Ferrari would win the 24 Hours of Le Mans race.

They had Alberto Ascari, the current world champion, driving for them.

They also had the Ferrari 375 with the massively powerful 4.5 litre V12 engine.

The only other car that could even come close was the Jaguar C-type, but it only had a 3.4 litre straight-6 engine.

And, instead of the world champion, it had Duncan Hamilton and Tony Rolt driving.

And the day before the race, Hamilton and Rolt were disqualified on a technicality anyway.

They went to a bar to drown their sorrows.

And they carried on drowning their sorrows, in fact they were up all night drowning them.

They were still drowning them at breakfast when the owner of Jaguar, Sir William Lyons, found them and said he'd agreed to pay a FF25,000 fine, they were racing in six hours.

Well even if the car was okay, they weren't.

They hadn't slept, they hadn't sobered up, and they had six hours to face the best in the world in a 24-hour race.

They did the only thing they could, they drank coffee and brandy, and at pit stops they drank more coffee and brandy.

And both stimulants seemed to have worked.

They broke the lap record, they broke the windscreen, the driver even broke his nose.

They raced for a day and a night against the best in the world and they won.

They won Le Mans by four laps, half an hour ahead of the next car to finish.

They were the first drivers ever to average over 100 mph for the entire 24 hours.

It's tempting to ask: **"If coffee and brandy work so well why doesn't every driver take it before and during every race?"**

Well the truth is, it wasn't just the coffee and brandy that the drivers had.

It was also something the car had: disc brakes.

Disc brakes were brand new at that time, and the other racing cars didn't have them.

Slowing down a car wasn't what racing was about, going faster was what racing was about.

That's why Ferrari had a bigger, more powerful engine.

But that is only one kind of thinking, in fact that's straight-line thinking.

And no racetrack is a straight line, they are loops, with bends.

However fast you are going on the straight you will need to slow down for the bends.

And the faster you are going the more you need to brake.

This was the creative part of Jaguar's thinking.

Ferrari, like all the other cars, used drum brakes.

Drum brakes have the brake pads on the *inside* pushing outward to slow the wheel down.

Dunlop had developed disc brakes which have the brake pads on the *outside* pushing inward to slow the wheel down.

Because the drum pads are on the *inside* they get hotter, with no way to disperse the heat.

But the disc pads are on the *outside*, the air rushing past cools them down straight away.

Heat is what stops brakes from working, if they can't get rid of the heat they fade.

Disc brakes get rid of the heat fast, drum brakes don't.

So the disc brakes meant the Jaguar could consistently out-brake the Ferrari, turn after turn.

Which is exactly what they did for 24 hours.

The Ferraris had to slow down for the corners because their brakes would fade.

The Jaguars went through the corners faster because their brakes *didn't* fade.

Jaguar changed the game so that all the power Ferrari had under the bonnet didn't matter.

It was the dawn of a new type of creative thinking about winning races.

That's why when Colin Chapman, the founder of Lotus cars, was asked why he concentrated on lightness instead of power, he said:

"Adding power makes you faster on the straight.

Subtracting weight makes you faster everywhere."

It's worth remembering that for everyone who likes to call themselves creative.

Don't just try to be better than other people, be different.

WOKE v JOKE

The Cambridge Union was debating the motion: 'This House Believes There is No Such Thing as Good Taste'.

400 students were in the audience to hear art historian Andrew Graham-Dixon present his view, 'Bad Taste and Bad Morality go Hand-in-Hand'.

To make his point, he parodied Hitler, in a bad mock-German accent he said:

"Zis modern, horrible art zat vos promoted by ze Jews ... it vos cubist – inspired by ze art of ze negro. Zis tribal art, urgh, how horrible is zat? Ve must expunge it from Deutschland. Ve are pure, Aryan people. Our genetics is pure, our taste must be pure."

Not a terribly witty speech maybe, but obviously a piss-take.

It went down quite well, in fact he won the debate.

But the next day the Cambridge Union received a large number of complaints.

At which point Cambridge Union President Keir Bradwell decided to take action.

He said, **"We will create a blacklist of speakers never to be invited back to the Cambridge Union, and we will share that blacklist with other unions. Andrew Graham-Dixon's name will be on that blacklist."**

Graham-Dixon then did the typical thing for someone who sees their livelihood threatened by cancellation, he immediately issued an apology.

"I apologise sincerely to anyone who found my debating tactics and use of Hitler's own language distressing; on reflection I can see that some of the words I used, even in quotation, are inherently offensive."

So far, so normal: joke – offence – cancellation – apology.

But then an unusual thing happened, instead of taking the cancellation seriously and being terrified of it, someone decided to ridicule it.

John Cleese sent the following tweet (he has 5.6 million followers):

"I was looking forward to talking to students at the Cambridge Union this Friday, but I hear that someone there has been blacklisted for doing an impersonation of Hitler. I regret that I did the same on a Monty Python show, so I am blacklisting myself before someone else does."

He followed it with another tweet:

"I apologise to anyone at Cambridge who was hoping to talk with me, but perhaps some of you can find a venue where woke rules do not apply."

By cancelling himself, John Cleese completely turned the tables.

Louis de Bernières, the author of **Captain Corelli's Mandolin**, immediately demanded to be put on the blacklist as well.

Being put on the blacklist suddenly became a badge of honour, young comedians wanted to be included on it, Ian McEwan and Tom Stoppard expressed their support.

Suddenly the situation was reversed and Keir Bradwell issued another statement: **"The Cambridge Union does not have a blacklist, I mis-spoke and should not have used that term. Further guests may say what they wish in our chamber, and absolutely never need to fear that anything they say will put them on a list of any sort.**

Obviously announcing a U-turn looks silly. I was just a 21-year-old who tried to make the situation better. There is no policy to ban anyone for what they say – it's a free speech institution. If there is a dichotomy between free speech and offense, I will defend free speech. I don't want to create an impression that the Union is against free speech."

What that demonstrates for me is that, just because someone objects to something, it doesn't mean they're automatically right, it doesn't even mean they've given it much thought.

This includes any critics: trade publications, ASA, IPA, Clearcast, planners, account men, clients, other creatives, even sometimes yourself.

It also demonstrates that taking the piss is often more powerful than taking it seriously.

So we may not need to issue an automatic apology.

We shouldn't have a knee-jerk reaction to a knee-jerk reaction.

CHANGING THE GAME

The British very nearly lost the Second World War.

Not in any big single battle, but in a fight that dragged out for the length of the war.

Britain is comparatively small and can't feed its population.

Being an island, it can't get any supplies via road or rail, everything must come by sea.

So stop the ships bringing food and the country starves.

And that's very nearly what the U-boats did, they sank 2,779 ships, that's 14 MILLION tons.

The British formed the cargo ships into convoys of up to 60 ships for the navy to protect.

But a convoy has to move at the speed of the slowest ship.

This sometimes meant the entire convoy travelled at about 10 mph, an easy target for U-boats assembled in wolfpacks of 12 or 15.

Royal Navy destroyers stuck close to the convoy and chased a U-boat when it attacked, but that was too little, too late, fighting defensively wasn't working.

In 1941, the British were losing 50 merchant ships for each U-boat sunk.

And then Captain Walker had an idea (his crew nicknamed him 'Johnnie' after the whisky).

This is the point where he changed the game by thinking upstream.

He said: **"The problem is we've been thinking of the convoys as the prey. They aren't the prey, they're the bait. The U-boats are the prey."**

Walker's attitude was very simple – if he could sink the U-boats *before* they sank any ships, he wouldn't have to defend the convoys.

So he invented the hunter-killer group.

Until that point, the prime directive of the admiralty had been: **"The safe and timely arrival of the convoy."**

Johnnie Walker issued a different order to his ships:

"The object is to destroy U-boats, particularly those which menace our convoys. But our main object is to kill, and all officers must fully develop the spirit of vicious offensive. No matter how many convoys we may shepherd through in safety, we shall have failed unless we slaughter U-boats. All energies must be to this end."

He knew he'd never find U-boats by searching all over the Atlantic, but he knew the wolfpacks would be attracted to the convoys.

And he knew they'd have to form up together before they attacked.

He knew the wolfpacks would be gathering ahead of the convoys and lying in wait.

So he knew where to find the U-boats.

All he had to do was get to the wolfpack before the convoy did.

Hit them on the surface with bombs and gunfire, and when they dived with depth charges.

Which is exactly what he did, and in just one voyage he destroyed six U-boats.

His aggressive tactics were so successful that, by the end of the war, 781 U-boats had been destroyed.

Which eventually allowed the Allies to win the war.

All because Johnnie Walker got upstream and changed the game.

So what can we learn from history?

Well simply, that's how the best thinking works everywhere.

As Buddha said: **"Act, don't react."**

Get upstream and change the game.

Upstream thinking in business would include: how Volkswagen beat Detroit, how Avis took on Hertz, how Hertz responded, Alfred Hitchcock versus Hollywood, Rupert Murdoch versus Fleet Street, Steve Jobs and Apple, Jeff Bezos and Amazon, Phil Knight and Nike, and many more.

We can learn a lot by studying case histories like these.

Remembering of course that case histories are always written by the winners.

And winners always have the same motto: **"Don't play the game, change the game."**

DON'T GO WITH THE FLOW

Between 1975 and 1985, several nuclear power plants were built in Japan.

It's worth comparing two of these: Fukushima and Onagawa.

Fukushima was built by Tokyo Electric Power Company (TEPCo), Onagawa was built by Tohoku Electric.

TEPCo's focus was on building as efficiently as possible, wasting the least money.

Their only safety concern was earthquakes, so they built on a hard rock base by the sea.

All major equipment would be delivered by ship, but there was a high wall of rock between the plant site and the sea, so the rock wall was blasted away.

35 miles away, the Onagawa nuclear power plant was to be built.

Similarly, it was built on a hard rock base next to the sea.

But the main difference between the two companies was a man named Yanosuke Hirai, vice-president of Tohoku Electric.

Hirai remembered a shrine he visited as a child, dedicated to the people killed in a massive tsunami 1,000 years before.

So, because he was vice-president, he was able to insist that the site be moved inland to another site of solid rock 50 feet above sea level.

He also insisted a sea wall be built 50 feet high, even though everyone insisted 30 feet was more than adequate.

And, because he knew that before a tsunami all the seawater recedes, he had emergency systems built to make sure there was always enough water for the cooling system.

Everyone thought it was a ridiculous concern, what a waste of money.

No one could understand his obsession with tsunamis, any sane person would concentrate on earthquakes.

But, against all objections, Hirai insisted and Onagawa was built to be tsunami-proof.

In 2011, it seemed the conventional view was right, there was an earthquake at sea, near both power plants.

Fukushima survived the earthquake, but it didn't survive what happened next.

The earthquake caused the biggest tsunami in Japan's history.

The waves that came ashore were up to 100 feet high, 20,000 people died and 160,000 were made homeless.

The Fukushima power plant was destroyed, but the Onagawa power plant was unharmed.

In fact it was the only thing left standing in the area, the local people made homeless by the tsunami sought shelter there.

And this, despite the fact that Onagawa was 35 miles closer to the earthquake than Fukushima, so the tsunami that hit it was bigger.

Kiyoshi Kurokawa, the chairman of the NAIIC (the official body investigating the disaster) said the following: **"The accident at the Fukushima Daiichi Nuclear Power Plant cannot be regarded as a natural disaster. It was a profoundly man-made disaster that could, and should, have been foreseen and prevented."**

He blamed **"the Japanese mind-set of obedience and reluctance to question authority."**

It's good to register that.

At one nuclear plant everyone just went along with conventional wisdom, no one wanted to look stupid, and they ended up looking a lot worse.

At the other power plant one man stood alone, no one agreed with him, they mocked him, but in the end he was the only one who didn't look stupid.

It's worth remembering that when we're given a brief that doesn't make sense.

We can keep quiet and hope we don't look stupid.

Or we can question it, knowing that everyone else in the room probably thinks the same but they're frightened of looking stupid.

One way looks stupid, the other way really *is* stupid.

RING THE BELL

When he made his first film, **The Producers**, everyone told Mel Brooks he was crazy.

Joke after joke was in the worst taste, laughing at Nazis, laughing at Hitler.

They tried to get him to leave out the most extreme gags, like the overhead Busby Berkeley shot of a dancing swastika.

Brooks said: **"You don't walk up to the bell unless you're gonna ring it"**, and he left it in.

The studio heads were disgusted, they said the public wouldn't stand for it.

With no advertising, they showed the film in one cinema in Philadelphia, and without advertising there was no audience, just the seven studio heads.

None of them laughed and they walked out in silence.

The film was put aside and forgotten.

Mel Brooks said his film career was over, it was: **"The worst night of my life."**

A year later, Paul Mazursky was making a film with Peter Sellers.

Sellers was bored and decided they should hold a film club every week.

They'd get together at Charles Aidikoff's screening room, one of them would choose a film and provide the appropriate food.

Sellers went first with **Pather Panchali** by Sanjit Ray, and brought tandoori chicken.

Mazursky said next week he'd show Fellini's **I Vitelloni** and his wife would make spaghetti.

But when next week came there was a mix-up, Mazursky thought Aidikoff would get the film, Aidikoff thought Mazursky was bringing the film.

So there was no *I Vitelloni* by Fellini.

Mazursky said: **"Well we got the food, we gotta see something, what have you got in the projection room?"**

Aidikoff said: **"Nothing really, just a can of film lying around nobody wants."**

Sellers said: **"Never mind, put it on, just so we've got something to watch."**

And Charles Aidikoff began playing *The Producers.*

No one said anything, then they began smiling, then giggling, then falling around and screaming with laughter.

At the end of the film, Peter Sellers ran to the phone and began dialling friends to tell them he'd just seen the greatest comedy film in decades.

The next day Peter Sellers took out whole-page ads in the film-trade magazines:

"Last night I saw the ultimate film: *The Producers.*

Brilliantly written and directed by Mel Brooks, it is the essence of all great comedy combined in a single motion picture.

Without any doubt, Mel Brooks displays true genius in weaving together tragedy-comedy, comedy-tragedy, pity, fear, hysteria, schizophrenia, inspired madness and a largess of lunacy with sheer magic. The casting was perfect.

Those of us who have seen this film and understand it have experienced a phenomenon which occurs only once in a life span."

Those ads inspired the Fine Arts Theatre in New York to run the film.

Film lovers who read the trade papers queued around the block.

Word spread so fast that anyone who was anyone had to see it.

Mel Brooks won an Oscar, presented to him by Frank Sinatra.

The Producers was converted into a stage play, which had a six-year run on Broadway.

The stage play was converted back into another version of the film.

Nearly all Mel Brooks' subsequent films were in the top ten box-office earners in their year: *The Twelve Chairs, Blazing Saddles, Young Frankenstein, Silent Movie, High Anxiety, History of the World (part one), Spaceballs, Robin Hood: Men in Tights.*

So the point is, ignore the people who tell you they know what the public thinks, they don't.

Don't take them seriously.

In fact, we're better at our jobs when we don't take anything too seriously.

Or, as Mel Brooks said in his Oscar acceptance speech: **"I'll just say what's in my heart: ba-boom, ba-boom, ba-boom, ba-boom."**

CURE FOR DEPRESSION

IBM's President, Thomas Watson, was a dynamic man and revolutionised the company.

His motto, for every single employee, was **"THINK"**.

Which became very relevant in 1929, when the stock market crashed.

It was the most devastating stock market crash in history and signalled the start of the worldwide **'great depression'**.

Half the banks in America failed, unemployment was 20%, and industrial production dropped by 50%.

Most businesses were laying off workers, it was the sensible thing to do.

But when Watson called his top executives into the boardroom, he said:

"Gentlemen, some of our people have had to give a lot of thought to their finances, which has distracted their attention from the main issue, which is, of course, building IBM and making it a bigger and better business.

I have not done anything in the interests of IBM for the last three weeks, I have not talked with any of you about sales, money collections, etcetera.

Because I have been running a stockbroker's office for the last three weeks."

Watson was saying that they were all paralysed because all they were worrying about was the plummeting share price and their savings.

He knew worrying wouldn't solve anything, they needed to act.

So Watson did the opposite of what every other company was doing.

He didn't lay anyone off, he kept all the factories open, producing IBM machines.

And he did something no one had done before, he took 6% of revenue ($1 million then, $18 BILLION today) to build the first corporate research laboratory, and put all the inventors and engineers in the same building.

It looked crazy, inventory stockpiled and the share price plummeted.

But, unlike everyone else, Watson knew the depression couldn't last, and he wanted IBM to be better placed than anyone else when it finally ended.

Then, in 1933, Franklin Roosevelt was elected President.

Under his **'New Deal'** he passed the Social Security Act: employers would have to make deductions from every worker's wages so that the elderly, unemployed, disabled, and widows with children would get financial assistance.

Suddenly, every employer needed to keep track of the wages and hours of every single worker in the country, and so did the government.

Suddenly, every company needed lots of tabulating and calculating machines, now.

And there was only one company in full production on those machines, and with a massive inventory, ready to supply straight away: IBM.

For Woolworth's alone the cost was $250,000 a year ($4.5 BILLION today).

Between 1935 and 1939, IBM revenue increased by 81% and continued to climb for 45 years.

IBM didn't just dominate the market, they owned it.

During that period they invented the floppy disk, the barcode, the hard drive, and the ATM as we know it today.

Today, IBM employs 350,000 people worldwide, and IBM employees have won five Nobel Prizes.

All because, in 1929, Thomas Watson followed his own dictum: **"THINK"**.

As he said, himself, at the depths of the depression: **"When is industrial progress going to start again? I say it never stopped. You are going to find that inventive genius, progressive ideas, progressive people, have been more active than ever. Industrial progress never stops."**

Or, as Bill Bernbach would later say: **"It may well be that creativity is the last legal unfair advantage we are allowed to take over the competition."**

SCHOOL v WORLD

My son was studying graphics and advertising at St Martins.

He'd just finished his second year and had one more year to go.

We were talking about how to spend the summer holidays.

I said, **"If you're smart, you'll act as if you've already graduated and need a job in advertising.**

You'll spend the summer trying to get a job.

You won't get one of course, but in failing you'll learn how tough it is.

And you'll learn what you need to do in your final year in order to get a job when you do graduate.

So you'll be a year ahead of everyone else."

I told him I'd Xeroxed my portfolio and mailed out 50 copies to get my first job.

He thought he had a better idea than that.

He made a website and emailed out 600 copies, CDs and ECDs.

Most people deleted it unread of course.

But from that he got five placement offers.

One of those was with Ed Morris, who was ECD at Lowe.

After a month on placement, Ed offered him a job: result.

But when college started again, my son wanted to finish his degree.

So I said why not do both, see if you can work it out with Ed.

He said to Ed, **"I get three weeks holiday a year. Instead of taking it in one lump, can I take half a day off a week instead?**

That will allow me to go into college for the weekly crit."

Ed said fine, as long as he still did all the agency work.

But after a few months, his college found out he was working and gave him an ultimatum.

Either he had to quit the job or he had to quit college, he couldn't do both.

He said to me, **"What do I do Dad?"**

I said, **"Well, what's the purpose of going to college?"**

He said, **"To get a job."**

I said, **"Okay, you've got a job, so why do you need college?"**

He said, **"Well after all this work, I'd like to get my degree."**

I said, **"Okay, then think creatively, go and talk it over with Ed."**

Like all creatives, Ed doesn't like being told what to do by people in authority.

Ed said, **"Fuck 'em. Take as much time off as you need, as long you do all your work here.**

Tell them you've quit the job, and if they ask me I'll back you up."

And that's what happened.

He told his college he'd quit the job.

College work isn't nearly as tough as real work, and he was able to do it at weekends.

Meanwhile, to pay Ed back, he worked harder than ever on agency work during the day and evenings.

He kept the job and he got his degree.

But I think something much more important than that.

He learned how not to let other people write your agenda for you.

He learned how to out-think people and situations.

He learned that creativity is about taking advantage of people who are sticking rigidly to the letter of the law.

He got an education in the real world, not just the college world. Getting a result instead of just ticking boxes.

He got an education in real creativity.

PART 4

WHERE DO IDEAS BEGIN?

THE FIVE WHYS

When children begin to talk, one of the first things they continually ask is: **"WHY?"**

And when you give them an answer, their response is: **"WHY?"**

There seems no end to the number of times they can ask: **"WHY?"**

Until eventually the parent gets fed up and just says: **"Because I say so, that's why."**

This doesn't satisfy the child, but it does end the conversation.

However, there's actually something very useful in this basic instinct for enquiry.

For instance, at Amazon, Jeff Bezos was meeting with the leadership team, when the safety manager explained that an employee just had an accident.

Bezos said, "Stop right there." He walked over to a whiteboard saying he was going to show them all how he wanted everyone to start thinking, using 'THE FIVE WHYS'.

First he asked the safety manager: **"WHY did the employee injure his thumb?"**

The answer was, he got it caught in the conveyor.

Then Bezos asked: **"WHY did he get his thumb caught in the conveyor?"**

The answer was, he was trying to grab his bag which was on the conveyor.

Then Bezos asked: **"WHY was he trying to grab his bag?"**

The answer was, he put it on the conveyor which was switched off, but it got turned on.

Then Bezos asked: **"WHY did he put his bag on the conveyor?"**

The answer was, he used it as a table because there was nowhere else to put it.

That was it, Jeff Bezos had just demonstrated a simple (almost childlike) method of discovering the root cause of a problem.

So Bezos then had tables placed in all the areas near the conveyors.

Sakichi Toyoda, the founder of Toyota, developed THE FIVE WHYS.

It's so simple it's seemingly childlike, but Toyoda found this a strength, not a weakness.

The simplicity is what made it clear, memorable, and practical.

The real strength of this method is that it doesn't just provide a solution to the immediate problem, it identifies the root cause, so countermeasures can prevent it happening again.

Problems are often symptoms of deeper issues and this discipline stops people jumping to conclusions and getting locked into pre-formed answers.

The Lincoln Memorial was an illustration of this, it began to deteriorate and instead of jumping to conclusions, they used THE FIVE WHYS.

Q1) **"Why is the memorial deteriorating faster?"**

A) It gets washed more often.

Q2) **"Why does it get washed more often?"**

A) It has more bird droppings.

Q3) **"Why does it have more bird droppings?"**

A) More birds are attracted to it.

Q4) **"Why are more birds attracted to it?"**

A) Because it has more insects.

Q5) **"Why does it have more insects?"**

A) They are attracted by the constant lights.

So they turned the lights on later and got an immediate 85% decrease in bird droppings.

We should use the simplicity, the discipline and clarity of the FIVE WHYS in our jobs.

Our problems stem from the fact that we see simplicity as weakness and complexity as superior intellect.

So we jump swiftly to conclusions and miss out the gradual, logical process.

We would rather be wrong faster than right more slowly.

We are addicted to the appearance of intelligence rather than getting the right answer.

Consequently, because we jump to conclusions, we miss out the possibility of interesting, unexpected, or more creative solutions.

Because we jump to conclusions we arrive at obvious, conventional answers.

Our ego values speed and the appearance of intelligence, which leads to flawed thinking.

We value the process above the result, the means above the end.

Which really isn't very smart at all.

THE BIG IDEA STARTS IN THE BRIEF

When she was young, Nora Ephron thought writing was solely about writing.

At high school, she learned that writing, like most things, is much more about thinking.

She tells the story like this:

"My high school journalism teacher, whose name is Charles O. Simms, is teaching us to write a lead – the first sentence or paragraph of a newspaper story.

He writes the words 'Who What When Where Why and How' on the blackboard.

Then he dictates a set of facts to us that goes something like this: 'Kenneth L. Peters, the principal of Beverly Hills High School, announced today that the faculty of the high school will travel to Sacramento on Thursday for a colloquium in new teaching methods. Speaking there will be anthropologist Margaret Mead and Robert Maynard Hutchins, the President of the University of Chicago.'

We all sit at our typewriters and write a lead, most of us inverting the set of facts so that they read something like this: 'Anthropologist Margaret Mead and University of Chicago president Robert Maynard Hutchins will address the faculty on Thursday in Sacramento at a colloquium on new teaching methods, the principal of the high school Kenneth L. Peters announced today.' We turn in our leads. We're very proud.

Mr Simms looks at what we've done and tosses everything into the garbage.

He says: 'The lead to the story is: "There will be no school on Thursday."'

An electric light-bulb turns itself on in my head. I decide at that moment that I want to be a journalist."

What Nora Ephron's teacher demonstrated to them was that writing isn't about writing.

Writing, like everything, is about thinking.

All the students had done was to change the style of what he said, it hadn't occurred to them to think any deeper, they all went on auto-pilot and rewrote what he said.

But if they'd been thinking they'd have known 'faculty' means the teaching staff at school.

If there aren't any teaching staff at the school there can't be any school on that day.

And that's much more interesting, that takes the story to a whole new level.

Taking a boring set of facts to whole new level is what we should be doing, before we pick up a pencil or a marker, before we start tapping on a laptop, before we look on YouTube.

And that should really happen at the brief stage.

Don't just write the facts on a brief and hope someone does something stylish with it.

I saw this in action one particular time at GGT on the London Docklands account.

Docklands was 8 square miles of mud and rubble east of Tower Bridge.

It was a development area that no one wanted to build on because other development areas, like Milton Keynes and Peterborough, made themselves look more attractive with green fields, cows and sheep, and happy families in their ads.

Steve Henry and Paul Grubb looked at the brief and thought: if they've got green fields and cows that's because they're out in the country.

But you don't want to build an office block for your company out in the country.

So they wrote the campaign line: LONDON DOCKLANDS. WHY MOVE TO THE MIDDLE OF NOWHERE WHEN YOU COULD MOVE TO THE MIDDLE OF LONDON?

Using exactly the same facts, they reframed the other development areas to look dull and unprofessional by comparison.

They made them seem okay for leisure, but not for business.

So most big companies switched and started building their new offices in Docklands.

And now Docklands has some of the tallest building in Europe, and Milton Keynes and Peterborough still have green fields and cows.

Let's learn from Nora Ephron's teacher: writing a brief isn't about writing, it's about thinking.

PULP FACT

Used properly, the Socratic method is especially useful at briefing stage.

The method is to state a position, question the position by stating an exception, arrive at a new position, then repeat, until eventually we reach a point which Socrates calls 'aporia', or opening our mind to new possibilities.

There's a good example of its use in Quentin Tarantino's **Pulp Fiction**.

Jules says Marsellus Wallace overreacted when he threw Antoine Roccamora out the window for giving his wife a foot rub.

Vincent Vega disagrees: **"I hafta say, play with matches, ya get burned. You don't be giving Marsellus Wallace's new bride a foot massage. Antoine probably didn't expect Marsellus to react like he did, but he had to expect a reaction."**

Jules: **"It was just a foot massage, a foot massage is nothing."**

(Jules stated a position. Vincent Vega then states a contradiction.)

Vincent: **"It's laying hands on Marcellus Wallace's new wife in a familiar way. Is it as bad as eating her out – no, but you're in the same fuckin' ballpark."**

(Jules then rejects Vincent's exception.)

Jules: **"Stop right there. Eatin' a bitch out and givin' a bitch a foot massage ain't even the same fuckin' thing. It ain't no ballpark either. Foot massages don't mean shit."**

(This causes Vincent to prepare an exception to Jules's view to make his point.)

Vincent: **"Have you ever given a foot massage?"**

Jules: **"Don't be tellin' me about no foot massage – I'm the fuckin' foot-massage master."**

(Vincent makes a point that Jules must accept. Then Vincent raises an exception.)

Vincent: "Have you ever given a guy a foot massage?"

Jules: "Fuck you. Just because I wouldn't give no man a foot massage, don't make it right for Marcellus to throw Antoine off no building."

(Jules must accept the point, so Vincent drives it home.)

Vincent: "I'm not sayin' he was right, but you're saying a foot massage don't mean nothing and I'm saying it does. We act like they don't but they do.

There's sensual things going on that nobody talks about, but you know it, and she knows it, fuckin' Marsellus knew it, and Antoine shoulda fuckin' known better."

Jules raised a point he felt was beyond question, Vincent raised an exception, which caused a reappraisal because there were gaps in Jules's thinking.

This is something we could do with more of in our business, especially at briefing stage.

Robin Wight used to say that, at WCRS, they would pull at the brief like a dog with a piece of cloth.

If it held, the brief was sound, if it began to come apart it wasn't.

But we don't interrogate briefs because the people who write them don't want them questioned.

So let's consider the Magna Carta, in 1215 it was decreed that no one was above the law, even those who made the law.

By that standard, if the planners and strategists can question the creative work, creatives should be able to question the briefs.

And the starting point for creative questions is always the Bauhaus mantra: 'Form Follows Function'.

Does the desired FUNCTION of the brief derive from the stated FORM of the brief?

This fits very well with the Socratic method.

A good example of it was at BMP with the managing director, David Batterbee, and planner, Jim Williams.

We were pitching on the COI's Fire Prevention account, the particular problem was chip-pan fires.

Until that point the COI had done what they always did, shown the after-effects of a fire.

This had no effect, which was why the account was up for pitch.

Stage one of their thinking was that you prevented fires by showing how terrible they were.

Using the Socratic method, David and Jim questioned this: how would they know if the campaign was successful – how would they measure it?

The obvious answer was of course the number of chip-pan fires would go down.

But in Socratic style they persisted with the question: how will they measure if fires went down?

The only possible answer was, by the number of fire brigade callouts.

This led to Socrates' third stage, reframing the brief, which now became preventing fire brigade callouts, instead of just saying fires were bad, so how to do that?

The answer must be to tell people how to put out the fire themselves before they had to call out the fire brigade.

It sounds obvious now, but it was very different from the previous brief.

Instead of just negative ads scaring people, we did a positive campaign with useful information.

When it ran, the campaign put fire brigade callouts down by 40%, and got a D&AD award.

Just by persistent questioning of apparently locked-off thinking.

Socratic thinking may be 2,000 years old, but that doesn't mean it's out of date.

THE ADVERTISING ELEPHANT

Jainism is a very gentle religion.

One Jainist belief is there is no single right answer to everything.

It is called 'Syadvada Anekantavada', illustrated by the story of the blind men and the elephant.

A wise man arrives in a village where six blind men are arguing.

An elephant had walked through the village and they each had a second to stroke it.

The first blind man only felt the tusk, he said an elephant was like a spear.

The second blind man just felt the tail, he said an elephant was like a vine.

The third blind man just felt the trunk, and said an elephant was like a snake.

The fourth blind man only felt the side, he said an elephant was like a huge wall.

The fifth blind man just felt the ear, and said an elephant was like a large leaf.

The sixth blind man only felt the leg, and said an elephant was like a tree.

The blind men asked the wise man, because he could actually see the elephant, which of them was right.

The wise man said they were all right, but they were also all wrong.

They all understood part of the truth, but none of them understood the whole truth. Because none of them had seen the whole elephant, just their individual part of it, and they mistook that for the whole.

This simple story reminds me of a debate I often hear between planners and creatives.

Creatives say planners have ruined advertising by making it too complicated.

Planners say creatives don't care about effectiveness, just winning awards.

Like the elephant story, both are right and both are wrong.

Because mainly, planners and creatives don't see the big picture, just their part.

They, like account handlers and media, think their part is the whole thing, so they do their job in a vacuum.

None of them understand the complete picture of advertising.

Planners (aka strategists) think the whole job is to deliver a message about the brand.

Creatives think the whole job is an ad that stands out, stylishly and artistically.

Media think the whole job is to get as many insertions as possible in the most highly targeted spaces.

Account handlers think the job is to keep the client happy.

And it's true, all those are part of the job.

But none of those alone is the whole job, only together are they the whole job.

If we don't make original impactful advertising, no one will notice it or remember it.

So everything else will be wasted effort and money.

But if we don't get the brand messaging right, even if people notice and remember the ad, no one will remember who the ad was for or what it said.

And even if we get the brand messaging and the advertising right, but we run it under a railway bridge where no one can see it, then all that effort is wasted.

And of course, if the client hates the agency and takes the business somewhere else, then we don't get to do the advertising in the first place.

So all of those things are part of the answer that builds to great advertising.

The problem is, there's hardly anywhere where all those things happen, where everyone sees the whole elephant.

Impactful, memorable advertising, delivering the right message, in the most powerful, cost-effective media, with a happy, engaged client.

That's why it shouldn't be an argument between departments.

We should be training ad people who understand, and participate in, the whole job, not just one part of it.

When everyone understands how the separate parts fit together to create a whole, then we'll have great advertising.

WE DON'T NEED STRATEGISTS, WE NEED PLANNERS

In 1941, Japan made a huge mistake by attacking Pearl Harbour.

But what's more interesting is *why* they made such a big mistake.

They made that massive mistake because they thought it was a strategy.

But it wasn't a strategy, it was tactics.

Not understanding the difference between strategy and tactics is what makes decisions ineffective and pointless.

Put simply, strategy is the **WHAT**, tactics is the **HOW**.

Strategy is the end point, tactics is how to get there.

So, calling the attack on Pearl Harbour a strategy meant Japan saw that as a final outcome.

Of course it wasn't the final outcome, it was just the start.

But they gave no thought to what would happen next.

So there was no strategy, just tactics disguised as strategy.

Strategy has become a catch-all word for planning.

Tactics end when a *specific* objective is achieved, strategy doesn't end until the *overall* objective has been achieved.

The Americans had a strategy: work their way towards Japan island by island.

Every battle on the way was a tactical battle that would ultimately lead to the strategic end.

The casual misuse of the term strategy leads to sloppy, inefficient thinking.

By calling all tactical thinking strategic we aren't really thinking at all.

Every problem needs planning, it doesn't need strategic thinking.

That's why I'm sad to see planners calling themselves strategists.

Just the way I'm sad to see copywriters and art directors calling themselves creatives.

It gives each one an overblown sense of their own importance.

It relieves them of the burden of doing the job they're supposed to be doing: thinking.

Not every job needs a creative solution, many just need styling.

Not every job needs a strategic solution, most need a tactical solution.

What we actually need are planners who know the difference between strategy and tactics.

What sort of thinking is appropriate, and where?

Usually in agencies, most strategic thinking is done at the pitch.

That's where the agencies compete to come up with a winning *strategy* to take the client in a new direction.

On existing work, the strategy doesn't change every time a brief for a new ad comes in, or a piece of content, or social media, or whatever.

The daily running of an account might well require different tactics, it certainly doesn't require a different strategy.

So what use is a strategist in that situation?

In that situation you want a planner, someone who knows when and how to think creatively about short-term objectives, not just a grand strategist.

You want someone who can roll their sleeves up, someone who can think like a sergeant, not just like a general.

That's why a planner is much more use to me than a strategist.

Good planners are creative, and there's a shortage of that everywhere.

Churchill knew the difference, in 1941 in **A Roving Commission: My Early Life** he wrote:

"Writing a book is not unlike building a house or planning a battle or painting a picture.

The foundations have to be laid, the data assembled, and the premises must bear the weight of their conclusions.

In battle however the other fellow interferes all the time, and the best generals are those who arrive at the results of planning without being tied to plans."

THE ABILENE PARADOX

In 1974, Jerry B. Harvey wrote an article entitled: 'The Abilene Paradox: The Management of Agreement'.

It starts in Texas on a hot afternoon, a husband and wife and the wife's parents are sitting on the porch, reading.

The wife's father says: **"I've got a great idea, let's drive to a nice little restaurant I know in Abilene for dinner."**

The wife's mother says: **"What a good idea, that would be wonderful."**

The wife says: **"That sounds great, it would be a pleasant break."**

The husband says: **"Sure why not, it'll make a nice change."**

So they all get in the car and drive 60 miles, in the blistering heat, to Abilene.

When they get there, the restaurant isn't as nice as the father remembered, there is no air-conditioning, the food isn't great, and they're hot and sweaty from the long drive.

And now they have to get back in the car and drive all the way home.

When they finally get home again, the father says: **"Well, that was worth doing wasn't it?"**

The mother says: **"To tell you the truth it wasn't, I didn't enjoy it, I don't know why we went."**

The wife says: **"Me neither, I would have rather stayed here."**

The husband says: **"Me too, I only went because I thought you all wanted to go."**

The father says: **"Well I didn't want to go either, I only suggested it because I thought you were all getting bored just sitting on the porch."**

And so they had a situation that no one wanted and no one enjoyed.

They all went along with it because they each thought the others wanted it.

They weren't thinking what the best thing to do was.

They were just trying to guess what the others might think.

Instead of thinking of the best solution they were second-guessing someone else, and consequently got a solution no one wanted.

This is called the Abilene Paradox and we see it a lot in our business.

Usually when some exciting, unusual creative work is presented.

The usual response is: **"I don't think the client will buy this"** or: **"I don't think this is what the client is looking for."**

Because we're not judging the work itself, we're trying to second-guess the client.

So we're not asking **"Is the work great?"** we're looking for what they will be happy with.

So that becomes the target for our advertising, keep the client happy.

But this is short-term thinking.

Because when the ads don't work the client won't be happy.

And the client won't say: **"Fair enough it was my fault, I liked it but I was wrong."**

The client won't say that because that isn't the way the relationship works.

If the ads don't work it will be the agency's fault, not the client's.

So the agency will lose the account.

You see the real client is the consumer, and the real client happiness is on the sales chart.

When the client sees the sales figures then they will decide if they are happy or not.

And that's the Abilene Paradox for most agencies: by trying to keep their clients happy they end up losing the account.

Because trying to guess short-term client happiness is not the correct measure for great advertising.

And all the second-guessing does is ruin the advertising and guarantee failure.

Trying to do work to please the client makes that your goal, and it shouldn't be.

Ultimately, when the advertising doesn't work, the client won't be happy.

THERE ISN'T A RIGHT BRIEF

The Melbourne State Theatre is considered one of the finest places to stage an opera.

The acoustics are superb.

The stage is so lavish, the biggest productions can easily be accommodated there.

It's always held up as an example of the finest Australia can do in the way of producing a near-perfect venue for classical productions.

Now let me ask you a question: what does it look like?

Have a good think, is it square or round? Is it tall or short? Is it grey or brown?

Hold a picture of the Melbourne State Theatre in your head.

You can't? Funny, neither can anyone else.

Let me ask you another question: what does the Sydney Opera House look like?

I bet you've got an instant picture in your head: colour, size, shape, everything in detail.

Even if you've never been to Australia you know what it looks like.

Because it's an icon.

It's an icon like London's Big Ben, or New York's Chrysler Building, or Paris's Eiffel Tower, or the onion roofs of Moscow's St Basil, or Rio de Janeiro's statue of Christ, or Delhi's Taj Mahal.

Those buildings are so individual, so unusual, they are like logos for those cities – no other cities have anything like it.

Those other cities don't have an icon, a piece of architecture instantly recognisable to anyone around the world.

That's what makes the Sydney Opera House special, that was the brief.

But people keep faulting it by comparing it to the Melbourne State Theatre when it comes to actually putting on an opera.

To quote Brian Thompson, designer for Opera Australia: **"As a building, it's the greatest in the world. But as a theatre, it's the worst."**

When John Malkovich performed there, he said: **"It's lovely to drive by in a motorboat, but the acoustics are hideous."**

Daniel Robertson, conductor with the Sydney Symphony Orchestra, said: **"It's a huge space and the sound must be very beautiful up there, if you're hanging from the roof by a rope."**

In a poll of Australia's twenty major classical music venues, the Melbourne State Theatre came top and the Sydney Opera House came bottom.

Which is why they are frequently compared.

The Melbourne stage is a huge 46 metres. The Sydney stage is a tiny 19 metres.

The Melbourne wings are **"as big as a couple of football fields."** The Sydney wings are **"a couple of metres each side."**

The Melbourne orchestra pit is 88 square metres. The Sydney pit is 28 square metres.

And the sound in the Melbourne State Theatre is amongst the finest in the world.

So it looks like a win for Melbourne, well maybe, but that depends on the brief.

If the brief was to have wonderful acoustics in a building that no one outside Melbourne even notices, then they win handsomely.

But the actual brief was for an Australian architectural icon, a logo to stay top-of-mind with the most famous half-a-dozen cities in the world, and on that brief Sydney wins.

Neither brief is right or wrong, but I'm a big believer in **'form follows function'**.

That's why it's critical to get the brief right before you start.

Define the function, and stick to it.

So that afterwards, when people start to change the brief (and they will change the brief) you can always refer back to the original purpose, and the reason you did what you did.

Then they can't criticise it for what it was never meant to do.

TELL US WHAT, NOT HOW

Ranulph Fiennes was the first person to circumnavigate the globe by the polar route.

He was the first person to cross Antarctica on foot.

He was the oldest person to climb Everest, at 65.

He's completed countless endurance expeditions to inaccessible places.

But what impresses me most is his thinking.

He wants all the input he can possibly get, but he wants to take the decisions himself.

Because he'll be taking responsibility for the consequences.

He attempted to walk alone and unsupported to the North Pole, while dragging a sled with all his provisions.

The weak ice cracked and the sled fell through into the freezing water.

Fiennes had to use all his strength to haul the massive thing up out of the water.

The temperature was minus 50 and the fingers on his left hand were frostbitten.

Back home, the fingers turned black and gangrenous.

Fiennes asked the surgeon to cut them off, they were already dead.

The surgeon said he wanted to wait as long as possible.

Fiennes heard the surgeon's view but he didn't agree.

He couldn't stand the fact that the useless fingers kept knocking against things.

They were like lumps of wood stuck on the end of his hand.

So he went out to his garden shed and put his hand in the vice.

Then he took a saw and one by one cut off the fingers and thumb.

First he heard the surgeon's views, then he made his decision.

Several years later, he had a massive heart attack and needed a double heart bypass.

During his recovery, he became intrigued with the idea of running seven marathons, on seven continents, in seven days, just two months after his operation.

His wife, Jenny, insisted they ask the surgeon that operated on him.

The surgeon said: **"I've done this operation over two thousand times, but I've never been asked if someone can run even one marathon afterwards. So I have no experience."**

But the next thing the doctor said constitutes, for me, the essence of a great brief.

The doctor said: **"But whatever you do, do not let your heart rate go above 130 bpm."**

That is a great brief, all the information he needed, without telling him what to do.

His doctor didn't say: "Under no circumstances run a marathon."

The doctor just told him what he needed to do in order to stay alive.

So Fiennes was able to run the marathons and not let his heart rate get above 130 bpm.

Because he'd had an informative, useful briefing.

Ranulph Fiennes had been in the SAS, a special forces unit of the British Army specialising in counter-terrorism, hostage rescue, direct action, and covert reconnaissance.

Members were selected for their ability to use their initiative.

To think for themselves as circumstances changed.

To achieve unexpected results against superior forces.

They were given an objective but not told how to achieve it.

Why can't we be briefed like that?

Briefs that tell us WHAT to do but not HOW to do it.

But we don't trust the creative department to use their initiative.

We expect them to meekly take dictation without question.

Which means we hire people who are willing to take dictation without thinking.

Which could explain the results we are currently all complaining about.

Where I grew up there was an expression for not trusting someone to do a job.

I think it sums up marketing's approach to advertising.

The expression was: **"It's like having a dog and barking yourself."**

THE ANSWER IS BRAND, NOW WHAT'S THE QUESTION?

In the ancient Greek myth, Procrustes was a robber and murderer.

He would invite weary travellers to stay the night in his house and use his bed.

While they slept, he would tie them up and then make them fit the bed exactly.

If they were too tall, he would amputate their legs, if there too short he would stretch them on the rack.

Either way they eventually died, then he took their money and possessions.

This went on for many years until eventually, Theseus captured Procrustes.

He forced him to submit to the same treatment and of course it killed him.

Over the centuries the term **'Bed of Procrustes'** became shorthand for forcing anything, usually ideas or data, into a pre-formed conclusion.

Thinking would be stretched or shortened until it fitted the required answer.

The start point for the investigation wasn't the information gathered, and then working to discover a conclusion.

The start point was the required conclusion, then working backwards to make all the information fit, anything that didn't fit being altered or discarded.

The modern equivalent is the saying: "The answer is X, now what's the question?"

In the case of advertising, it would be: **"The answer is 'brand' now what's the question?"**

Brand is our Bed of Procrustes, it is so ingrained as an answer we can't even see it.

And yet several decades ago, brand didn't exist as an answer.

It was obvious that most of the reasons people bought things were: price, size, range, availability, design, efficiency, durability.

Right at the end of a long list was brand, it was only a small thing, but for marketing types it seemed to be the only part advertising could affect.

As it was the one thing advertising could control it was exaggerated in importance.

An entire department was built around brand, called the 'Brand Planning Department'.

And it was staffed by university graduates who couldn't do advertising, but they could write long papers on brand planning.

Which meant clients had to recruit graduates to decipher long papers on brand planning.

And pretty soon university graduates and brand planning took over from advertising.

The answer to every problem had to be cut or stretched until it fitted the solution **'brand'**.

Which meant advertising was reduced to an academic subject, like a thesis.

The answer always had to be brand, there was no other possibility, it had to be made to fit.

But is that always true?

A couple of decades ago the largest advertising spender in the country was the COI, Central Office of Information.

They had massive accounts like road safety and fire prevention.

Brand wasn't the answer to any of their requirements, behavioural change was.

It didn't matter if anyone found the brand **'road safety'** attractive, it only mattered whether they drove more safely and didn't kill so many people.

Another of the biggest spenders was the HEC, Health Education Council, which had accounts like anti-smoking.

It didn't matter whether anyone found the brand **'anti-smoking'** attractive, it only mattered whether they stopped smoking and fewer people died.

But it seems we're not interested in changing behaviour anymore, it doesn't fit with the answer **'brand'**.

So here's another thought, another way of approaching advertising.

Maybe there's an alternative to cutting up problems to fit the bed called **'brand'**.

Maybe we could have different size beds to fit different problems.

Just a thought.

WHY THE FIRST BRIEF IS WRONG AND LAZY

Recently I saw a post from someone called Annie, she said:

"Every time I have a programming question and I really need help, I post it on Reddit and then log into another account and reply to it with an obscenely incorrect answer.

People don't care about helping others, but they LOVE correcting others.

Works 100% of the time."

This is very smart on Annie's part, but it turns out Annie is using Cunningham's Law.

This was coined by Steven McGeady in 2010 and states: **"The best way to get the right answer on the internet is not to ask a question, it's to post the wrong answer."**

McGeady says he learned this from Ward Cunningham, the inventor of Wiki.

But Cunningham wasn't talking specifically about the internet, his advice was more general: **"People are quicker to correct a wrong idea than to answer a question."**

For us, this is very interesting: Bernbach says, in the communications business, **"Our proper area of study is simple, timeless, human truths."**

Sir Arthur Conan Doyle was a student of human nature, it's what gives his detective, Sherlock Holmes, an advantage over others.

In 'The Adventure of the Blue Carbuncle' Holmes needs information from a salesman.

The salesman refuses to help, so Holmes makes a bet with him that is clearly incorrect:

"I'm always ready to back my opinion on a matter of fowls, and I have a fiver on it that the bird I ate is country bred."

"Well, then, you've lost your fiver, for it's town bred," snapped the salesman.

"It's nothing of the kind."

"D'you think you know more about fowls than I, who have handled them ever since I was a nipper? I tell you, all those birds that went to the Alpha were town bred."

"You'll never persuade me to believe that."

"Will you bet, then?"

"It's merely taking your money, for I know that I am right. But I'll have a sovereign on with you, just to teach you not to be obstinate."

The salesman chuckled grimly. 'Bring me the books, Bill,' said he."

(The salesman opens the books he previously refused to open. Holmes inspects them, gets all the information he needs, then surrenders the sovereign.)

Later Holmes explains to Watson:

"When you see a man with whiskers of that cut and the 'Pink 'un' protruding out of his pocket, you can always draw him by a bet," said Holmes. "I daresay that if I had put £100 down in front of him, that man would not have given me such complete information as was drawn from him by the idea that he was doing me on a wager."

Holmes sums up the simple timeless human truth: **"People don't like telling you things, but they love to contradict you."**

The people who couldn't, or wouldn't, help you do the job will always tell you what's wrong with it after it's done.

For instance, the people who write the brief and can spot exactly what you should have put in the ad once you present the finished work.

Their suggestions weren't written in the brief where they would have been helpful *before* you did the work.

125

But after you've done the work, they are keen to say exactly what's wrong with it, and a new brief is issued.

Because it's more interesting to crit someone else's work than to put in the effort to do the job properly in the first place.

That's why it's important for creatives to question the brief before starting work on it.

As Robin Wight used to say, **"Creatives should tug at the brief like a dog pulling at a piece of cloth, if it holds it's good, if it comes apart it isn't."**

PART 5

WHO DECIDES WHAT'S AN IDEA?

WHAT IS BRAND?

I was at a friend's house and he had a beautifully framed object on the wall.

At least, the frame was beautiful and clearly expensive, the object in the frame was just a crumpled old Marlboro pack, bent and tatty, like you'd find in any gutter.

My friend proudly said **"It's signed by Tracey Emin",** so that explained it.

One minute it was just another piece of rubbish, but sign it and now it was a piece of art, worth a lot of money.

That's brand.

Picasso used to say that people didn't buy his paintings, they bought his signature.

Which is another way of saying they don't know what they're looking at, they just want something other people can recognise as being valuable.

Interestingly, Picasso usually paid for anything he bought with a cheque.

He saved a lot of money, because he knew that his signature made it more valuable for them to keep the cheque rather than cash it.

That's brand.

In Camden Town, Banksy sprayed some graffiti on a wall.

A jealous competitive graffiti artist came along and sprayed over Banksy's design.

The residents complained to the council, the Banksy had increased the value of their properties, now it was defaced.

The council had to have it renovated by a professional who put the Banksy back to its original state, and then put a protective shield over it.

That's brand.

Donald Trump has properties all over America, except he doesn't.

Most of those properties are owned by other people.

When they bought them it was on the agreement that they would keep the Trump name on the front of the buildings and pay a huge yearly fee for use of it because, to some people, it apparently conveys an image of wealth, fame, and glamour.

That's brand.

Often, when I do a speech, the organisers insist on me doing a book signing afterwards.

I sit at a desk with a pen because people are more likely to buy a book if it is signed.

I never understood this, I thought you buy a book for what's in it, but no, many people will pay extra for a book that's signed.

During Covid lockdown there weren't any book signing events.

So I see advertisements from authors offering to send signed sticky labels to people for books they bought during lockdown.

That's brand.

My friend, who lives in Surrey, tells me he sees neighbours shopping in Lidl and then putting what they've bought into Waitrose bags to carry home.

That's brand.

Volkswagen Touareg and Porsche Cayenne were virtually the same cars.

They were made by the same company, they had the same platform, they had many shared parts.

But the car with the Porsche badge cost £8,000 more than the car with the VW badge.

That's brand.

I saw this cleverly used in an American Express campaign years ago.

Their strapline was: **"American Express: It says more about you than cash ever can."**

Think of that, paying the exact same amount of money by credit card gave you a cachet that paying by genuine currency couldn't.

It made you seem more upstanding, more reliable, more trustworthy.

That's brand.

DRINKING THE LABEL

Lee Lantz was an American fish wholesaler.

He was constantly on the lookout for new kinds of fish to import.

This was difficult, as the most desirable fish were obviously in great demand.

Lantz knew what anyone involved in marketing knows, the answer is always in one of two places: the product or the consumer.

It's not a secret formula, you must have supply and demand: a good product and people who want it.

So the job is twofold: discover (or make) a good product, discover (or create) a demand.

In 1977, Lantz managed to tick the first box.

On a trip to Chile, he discovered the Patagonian Toothfish.

It was known amongst fishermen as **'trash fish'**, which meant when they caught it they tossed it back, because they couldn't sell it.

It was the ugliest fish he'd ever seen: huge googly eyes, a massive jutting lower jaw full of teeth, and it grew to be roughly the size of a human.

But that didn't matter to Lantz, no one needed to see the fish in its original state.

All the customer would see was the flesh, and the revelation for Lantz was the taste, it was white and creamy, rich buttery flakes that melted in the mouth.

He solved the first half of the equation, he'd found the product.

But the second part was the problem: demand, no one wanted something called a Patagonian Toothfish.

It sounded ugly and scaly, and full of bones and teeth, it sounded totally unappetising.

What Lantz had to do was solve the consumer problem, by making it appetising.

So he changed the name, he named it the **'Chilean Sea Bass'**.

Now it sounded fresh and salty, now it tasted of the ocean and being freshly caught.

And the identical fish that had been thrown back into the sea, became the most sought-after item on the menu.

Gourmet magazines wrote about this new discovery, restaurants like The Four Seasons and Nobu had to have it on their menu.

Establishments that wouldn't even sell it as Patagonian Toothfish, were now charging up to $50 for it as Chilean Sea Bass.

Over the next decade, demand for the renamed fish increased by up to 40 times, until overfishing became such a problem that it had to be regulated.

What Lantz had understood was what all chefs understand, presentation: before you eat a dish with your mouth, you eat it with your eyes.

Although in this case it was: you eat it with your ears.

The name creates the image, the image creates the taste.

There's a saying in beer advertising: you drink the label.

I used to teach students about this with a cigarette.

I'd hold it up in front of the class and say: **"Okay, this is a Dunhill King Size, before we taste it, what do we know about it, what's the image?"**

They'd shout out: **"Traditionally British"**, **"Bowler hats"**, **"Leather-top desks"**, **"Wing-back armchairs"**, **"Rolls Royces"**, **"Saville Row"**.

Then I'd look closely at the cigarette and say: **"Whoops sorry, I got the name wrong, it's Marlboro. Now what do we know about it."**

They'd shout out: **"Cowboys", "Saddles", "Belt buckles", "Cattle-drives", "Pickup trucks", "Country and Western music".**

Then I'd say: **"Okay I'm still holding the identical piece of tobacco and paper, but by changing the name we changed everything about it.**

And that's how brand works."

ALGORITHMS CAN'T DO CONTEXT

When I graduated art school I worked on a tramp steamer.

After a couple of weeks at sea, we stopped in Buenos Aires, to unload farm equipment and load coffee.

As the most junior deckhand, I was given the night watch.

I got chatting to a group of Argentine dock workers, well not chatting because I spoke no Spanish and they spoke little English.

But they were very friendly and we gathered round a bonfire in a big oil drum, warming our hands on a freezing-cold night.

One of them took out something like a small teapot, except it had no handle.

He filled it with some leaves, then he poured sugar on top, then he poured boiling water over it and put the lid on.

We passed it round one by one, taking turns sipping the hot drink through the spout.

I never tasted anything so good, when it was empty he poured more leaves on top, then more sugar and water, and we did it again.

They told me it was called yerba-maté, I thought I'd always drink it from then on.

But when the ship got back to New York, and I left it, I tried yerba-maté again and it didn't taste special at all.

I've often had that experience.

For instance, years back I was in Dublin, looking for a non-touristy pub.

I found a quiet one that was nearly empty, old wooden walls, sawdust on the floor.

The Guinnesses were lined up behind the bar, half-poured, waiting to be topped up.

As I drank mine I studied the old black and white photographs on the walls, of the siege at the Post Office in 1916, just two blocks away.

The sense of history was immense.

To say the Guinness was the best I ever tasted would be an understatement.

I spent the evening in that pub and resolved never to drink anything but Guinness again.

But when I got back to London, Guinness just tasted like any ordinary pint.

As I say, it's a phenomenon I often find.

Once I took away the docks, and the bonfire in the oil drum, and the camaraderie of the Argentine dock-workers, the yerba-maté lost 50% of its taste.

Once I took away the sawdust floor of the ancient Dublin pub, and the black and white photographs, and the history, the Guinness lost half its taste.

Because they'd lost their context, and half the taste is the context.

As the philosopher George Berkeley said: **"Esse est percipi"** – to exist, is to be perceived.

Or, as Buddha said, **"All there is, is mind."**

When you taste something, the tongue is the main experience, but it's not the entire experience.

Half the experience is the physical object, half is everything around it.

Doctors will tell you that a large part of any treatment is in the mind, which is why placebos often work so well.

That's why, in our terms, it's stupid to let algorithms alone decide the media.

All algorithms can tell you is how many eyeballs are in front of your ad, they can't tell you how the media affects the ad.

Years ago, our head of media planning, Julian Neuberger, told me that he could buy the same eyeballs more efficiently in the *News of the World* than the *Sunday Times*.

But where would a consumer durable, a watch or a car say, look like it's worth more: where are people more likely to spend time reading about it, which reflects better on the brand?

An algorithm can't tell you that.

Because algorithms don't understand anything except numbers.

CONVEYOR-BELT THINKING

In 1942, Antoine de Saint-Exupéry wrote a book called *The Little Prince*.

In it, he explains to children how adults think.

In the story, an asteroid, B-612, was discovered by a Turkish astronomer in 1909, but the Astronomical Society wouldn't believe him, because he was dressed in flamboyant Turkish clothes.

11 years later, in 1920, he again presented his evidence for asteroid B-612, but this time he was dressed in conservative western clothes, so they believed him.

Because adults are blind to anything not presented in the dullest possible way:

"When you tell them that you have made a new friend, they never ask you questions about essential matters.

They never say to you, 'What does his voice sound like? What games does he love best? Does he collect butterflies?'

Instead, they demand: 'How old is he? How many brothers has he? How much does he weigh? How much money does his father make?'

Only from these figures do they think they have learned anything about him.

If you were to say to the grown-ups: 'I saw a beautiful house made of rosy brick, with geraniums in the windows and doves on the roof,' they would not be able to get any idea of that house at all. You would have to say to them: 'I saw a house that cost $20,000.'

Then they would exclaim: 'Oh, what a pretty house that is!'"

Saint-Exupéry tells of the Little Prince, who originated on asteroid B-612, visiting Earth and trying to make sense of it.

He meets two people: the first is a railway switchman who tells him how passengers constantly rush from one place to another place aboard trains, never knowing where they were and not knowing what they were after, only the children among them ever bothered to look out of the windows.

The second person is a merchant who tells him about his product, a pill that eliminates the need to drink for a week, saving people 53 minutes.

The Little Prince says the people of Earth make no sense, just like those on other planets he's visited.

Such as the narcissistic man who only wants the praise which comes from admiration and being the most admirable person on his otherwise uninhabited planet.

Or the businessman who is blind to the beauty of the stars and instead endlessly counts and catalogues them in order to **'own'** them all.

But Saint-Exupéry wasn't talking to children, he was explaining us to us.

We don't care how we make anyone feel: do they laugh, do they remember it, can they sing it, would they watch it again?

All we care about is: did we tick all the research boxes, did we get the ratings, did we get an award, will we get mentioned in *Campaign*, will we get a raise?

Last night I was watching Sky TV, there were four ad breaks an hour, each ad break had 13 commercials – that's 52 ads, around 20 minutes, an hour.

The ads were targeted, so I saw the same ads over-and-over-and-over-and-over.

It's not only boring, it's suffocating.

Because we do our jobs the way Antoine de Saint-Exupéry described adults to children.

We can't judge good ideas, just facts presented in the dullest way.

Numbers and rules win every argument, anything else is considered trivia.

I felt this particularly poignantly this weekend.

Alan Parker died, he'd been an advertising giant when I was junior, before he went to Hollywood.

Everything the public loves and remembers from the great days of advertising was done by Alan and half-a-dozen others.

He did his final interview before he died, with Dave Dye, and his last answer struck home.

Dave Dye asked Alan what he thought of the present state of advertising.

Alan Parker said: **"When I see a Banksy on a wall I think: advertising used to be clever like that."**

TARGETING YOUR AUDIENCE

Many years ago I left work late; on the way out through reception I grabbed a paper to read on the tube.

As usual, the *Sun* had gone, the only paper left was the *Guardian*, no one wanted that.

So I took it and turned to the sports pages to read the West Ham write up.

I found the *Guardian* had a very different style of sports writing to the *Sun*.

I still remember what they wrote: **"Bonds and Lampard are the Scylla and Charybdis of the West Ham defence."**

I remember it because I didn't know what it meant.

I'd never heard of Scylla or Charybdis, obviously they played on some European team that only sophisticated *Guardian* sports writers knew about.

The sentence stuck with me, why hadn't I heard about them if they were that good?

Eventually I looked them up.

It turned out they weren't footballers at all, they were mythical sea monsters in ancient Greek mythology.

What did that have to do with a mid-week game at West Ham?

Well, according to Homer, Odysseus had to sail his ship between Sicily and the mainland.

To do that he had to pass between Scylla on one side and Charybdis on the other.

Scylla was a deadly group of rocks, depicted as a multi-headed sea monster, Charybdis was a whirlpool.

Basically, if one didn't get you then the other one would.

And that's what it had to with West Ham: **"Bonds and Lampard are the Scylla and Charybdis of the West Ham defence."**

If you tried getting past them, if one didn't get you then the other one would.

Of course, if the *Guardian* sports writer had written it like that I'd never have remembered it after all these years.

Which is a good thing to hold in mind about writing.

She could have written: **"With Bonds and Lampard you are on the horns of a dilemma."**

Or: **"Bonds and Lampard is a choice between the devil and the deep blue sea."**

Or: **"Bonds and Lampard is like choosing between a rock and a hard place."**

But she didn't, she wrote it that way because she considered her audience.

You couldn't mention Scylla and Charybdis in the *Sun* because *Sun* readers wouldn't have a clue (like me) what she's talking about.

But the *Guardian* isn't the *Sun*, all *Guardian* readers went to university, so they all know who Scylla and Charybdis are.

That's why the *Guardian* requires a more educated standard of writing than the *Sun*.

The *Sun* was a quick laugh for working people who liked a joke in a pub (like me).

The *Guardian* considered itself, and its readers, to be much more thoughtful.

Which is why even football must be presented differently in those two papers.

Same product, but different audience.

In the *Sun* it's tribal, in the *Guardian* it's genteel, I appreciate that.

I appreciate someone who can change gear according to the audience.

Most ordinary, working people aren't reading the *Guardian*, so you don't cater for them.

Ordinary people haven't got time to plough through acres of flowery language, they want the facts, fast.

But there are people who love what they consider quality writing.

We need to understand both, when and where they are appropriate.

We need to consider not just the product or brand, but more particularly the audience.

That's real targeting, that's our job.

Targeting is more than some automated media algorithm saying where the ads should run.

It's making sure we write different ads for different people in different media.

WHAT INFLUENCES THE INFLUENCERS?

In 2018, fashion bloggers were invited to the opening of a new store in LA.

Italian brand Palessi had taken over premises recently vacated by Armani.

It was to be Palessi's US launch, impossible to resist for anyone at the forefront of fashion.

It was invitation only, a private preview of their latest shoe range.

Until now, Palessi's shoes had only been available in Milan, Florence, and Rome.

The store was decorated in impeccable Italian taste: minimalist, mainly shades of grey, a single white statue of a winged lion, gold mannequins, shoes displayed like jewels.

Guests were served champagne and canapés by attractive young staff.

The influencers were so impressed, they video-blogged to their followers to show the sort of exclusive event they were invited to.

And they gushed about the shoes, in fact they couldn't wait to buy them.

Of course they weren't cheap, the prices were similar to Jimmy Choo, or Balenciaga, or Louboutin.

And the influencers paid up to $600 for their exclusive Palessi shoes.

After they bought them they were invited into a back room where it was explained to them that the shoes actually cost between $19.99 and $39.99 a pair.

Palessi was actually another name for Payless, the budget shoe store.

The entire event was being videotaped and, if they agreed to let Payless use the film for advertising, they could have their money back and keep the shoes for free.

Naturally, all the influencers quickly agreed.

And Payless had footage of fashion bloggers with thousands of followers saying the shoes were indistinguishable from the real thing.

Of course, if the influencers had refused, Payless would have had to give them their money back anyway, but the influencers didn't seem to spot that.

So Payless got fantastic advertising for next to nothing.

Does it mean that people who bought expensive shoes would now buy Payless instead?

Of course not.

The shoes are only a small part of what upmarket customers were paying for.

They're actually buying an exclusive brand, so what are they paying for then?

It's letting everyone know that they have shoes that only the richest people on the planet can afford, it makes them feel exclusive, discerning and special.

And of course, that isn't the Payless brand.

So what is the Payless brand, and who would buy that?

It's about value for money for the girl who wants to look as good as rich people but can't afford it, and wouldn't if she could.

It's smart shoes for no-nonsense people, with more sense than money.

Now would that advertising work amongst the Payless market?

Absolutely.

Those girls saw that all the people who routinely pay a fortune for shoes, the influencers who advise rich people, can't tell the difference.

So if you wear Payless shoes to a red-carpet event, no one would know.

Now that's a very different sort of brand.

And what I love is the agency realised people are different and want different things.

So brands have to be about different things.

Not just blindly following whoever else has been successful.

Even if they're successful, their market may have nothing to do with yours.

So before we even think about brands, we need to study the market.

Defining the brand can tell you where you currently are, but studying the market can tell you where you could go.

THE PENDULUM SWINGS BOTH WAYS

In 1649, Oliver Cromwell beheaded King Charles I.

Cromwell became lord protector, a dictator much more powerful than any king.

He banned all form of parties, singing, dancing, drinking, celebrations, even colourful dress.

No one dared argue, his rule was absolute.

When he died his body was buried in Westminster Abbey, as befitting any head of state.

But the pendulum began to swing the other way.

The king's son was reinstated, Cromwell's body was dug up and beheaded.

His head was stuck on a spike outside the House of Parliament where it stayed for 20 years.

Pendulums will eventually swing the other way.

In 1794, Maximilien Robespierre was the head of France's Committee for Public Safety.

He became more powerful than anyone in France, he oversaw 'the Terror'.

He had many people guillotined, no one dared oppose or even disagree with him.

But the pendulum began to swing the other way.

He was arrested and shot, before being guillotined himself and buried in an unmarked grave.

Pendulums will eventually swing the other way.

In 1922, Benito Mussolini became prime minister of Italy.

As a fascist, he ruled via fear and violence, everyone obeyed him without question.

But by 1943 the pendulum had begun to swing the other way.

He and his mistress were arrested and shot, their corpses were hung upside-down from a streetlight outside a petrol station.

Pendulums will eventually swing the other way.

In 1950, Senator Joseph McCarthy gave a speech in which he said 205 members of the communist party were working in the US government.

He drove a witch-hunt where anyone even suspected of being a communist was fired.

The entire country was in thrall to McCarthyism, scared to even whisper against him.

But by 1954, the pendulum began to swing the other way.

McCarthy was shunned by everyone; ignored and depressed, he became a pariah and drank himself to death.

Pendulums will eventually swing the other way.

In 1966, Jiang Qing became the chair of the Cultural Revolution Group.

She was Mao Zedong's wife and, after him, the most powerful person in China.

For ten years she oversaw the persecution of 730,000 people and the deaths of 35,000.

But in 1976, Mao died and the pendulum swung the other way.

She was arrested and sentenced to death.

It was commuted to life imprisonment but, in 1991, she hanged herself in the prison toilets.

Pendulums will eventually swing the other way.

Whatever the current orthodoxy, however much it can't be questioned, history teaches us it will eventually be reversed.

However deeply embedded it seems at the moment of its greatest power or influence.

Young people coming into advertising are desperate to learn whatever the current orthodoxy is because they assume it is the unchanging truth of advertising.

Brand-purpose, big data, ad-tech, behavioural science, wokeism, Millward Brown, Nielsen ratings, the Gunn report, interruption-is-dead, the campaign is dead, advertising is dead.

They don't realise it's just the prevailing view, the bandwagon everyone's jumping on.

It won't last forever, and where do you turn when the pendulum swings the other way?

Isn't it better to learn why advertising exists, what its real purpose is, not just the current fashion?

If you learn the truth of something you can hold onto it when fashions change.

You're not left clinging onto a pendulum that keeps swinging one way and the other.

A PICTURE IS WORTH A THOUSAND BOMBS

It was market day in a small town in the Basque part of Spain, Monday 26 April 1937, 4.30 in the afternoon.

The shoppers heard a rumbling overhead, they looked up and saw waves of Italian and German planes, objects began dropping out of the planes.

Some of the shoppers screamed and ran, but it didn't help, the objects were bombs.

The bombs were high explosives and they blew buildings apart, people either died in the explosions or were buried in the rubble.

As rescuers tried to get to the dead and injured, the second wave of bombers came over.

But these planes weren't dropping high explosives, they were dropping incendiary bombs.

Why did they drop high explosives first and fire bombs second?

Because the bombers were part of the Condor Legion, Germany's contribution to helping General Franco win the Spanish Civil War for the Fascists.

The Condor Legion was under the command of Oberstleutnant Wolfram von Richthofen, and the bombing was an experiment for the bigger war Germany knew was coming.

The objective was to find the most effective way of destroying a city.

So first they dropped high explosives, to shatter gas lines and create an inflammable atmosphere, to break water pipes so fire fighters couldn't put out fires, to create rubble to hamper emergency services, and to destroy electricity and phone lines so they couldn't co-ordinate a response.

Then, the second wave would drop fire bombs to ignite all that the gas and exposed wooden structures, and the broken water pipes would mean the fires couldn't be put out.

In this way the destruction was found to be more thorough and effective.

The lessons they learned that day were later used by the Germans over Britain, then by the British over Germany, then by the Americans over Japan.

300 people died in the bombing of that Basque town.

And yet, even today, it's much more famous than the bombing of all the other cities, where many, many thousands more died.

So why have more people heard of the bombing of this Basque town than any of the attacks on far larger cities?

It's because Picasso painted a picture named after that town, called 'Guernica'.

He painted it for the Spanish pavilion at the Paris International Exhibition in 1937.

It was 12 feet high by 26 feet long, painted in stark black and white, to feel more like a filmed documentary than a piece of art. A critic said of it:

"The protest is found in what has happened to the bodies, the hands, the soles of the feet, the horse's tongue, the mother's breasts, the eyes in the head – we are made to feel their pain with our own eyes."

Guernica, the painting, was exhibited in Denmark, Norway, Sweden, London, Liverpool, Leeds, Manchester, Brazil, Milan, New York, Chicago, San Francisco, and Philadelphia.

Nelson Rockefeller tried to buy it for the United Nations building in New York, but Picasso wouldn't sell the original, so Rockefeller had a huge tapestry commissioned to copy it.

Picasso stipulated that the painting could not be shown in Spain while it remained a dictatorship under Franco.

In 1975, Franco died and Spain was returned to democracy.

In 1981 the painting was returned to Spain and hung in the Museo Nacional del Prado in Madrid.

It had its own museum built and in its first year was visited by over a million people.

Of all the destruction in World War Two, one town is remembered more than any other because of one painting.

When we think of everything wrong in the world and we feel powerless to do anything about it, it's worth remembering the power of a single piece of creativity.

ADVERTISING ISN'T SWITZERLAND

In 2014, the *New York Times* had to lay off 100 newsroom staff.

Newspaper sales were down, people were getting their news and journalism online.

The owner made it clear, the journalists' job was no longer just to report the news, now it was to attract readers, because readers attract advertising revenue.

With the NYT moving online, it was able to economise via user-generated content.

Cooking features, games, plus live events, conferences, foreign trips, brands could even sponsor reporting, it was a long way from traditional journalism.

But what actually saved the NYT's bacon wasn't any of that.

It was the fight with Donald Trump.

Publicly, Trump and the *New York Times* despised each other: he always referred to them as **"the failing New York Times"** and **"fake news"**.

But Trump was the best thing that happened to them.

The liberal media published non-stop critical stories about Trump, in 2015 around $2 billion worth of free media, more than six times as much as any other candidate.

And stories about Trump sold more liberal media than anything else.

In a leaked tape, CNN (while publicly opposing Trump) was heard encouraging him to run and giving him tips on how to win a CNN sponsored debate.

The Chairman of CBS, Les Moonves, said, **"Trump may not be good for America but he's damn good for CBS."**

The more Trump hated the *New York Times*, the more the liberal elite wore it as a badge.

By 2016, the NYT had 276,000 digital subscribers (100,000 up on 2015).

By 2017, they had $340 million in online subscriptions (46% up on 2016).

By 2019, their digital-only subscribers totalled 5.2 million (up 1 million).

They reached $800 million, their digital revenue target for 2020, a year early.

In a fight, people are usually polarised towards one side or the other.

By demonising Trump, the NYT became compulsory reading for Trump haters.

By demonising the NYT, Trump was selling a lot of newspapers and online subscriptions.

The main learning for us is the opposite of current advertising thinking.

Our belief is that confrontation and controversy is a bad thing, we must avoid it at all costs, pull the offending ad immediately and apologise.

Staying quiet, not making a fuss, being neutral, not getting into trouble: this is exactly the opposite of the reason advertising exists.

That's exactly where the NYT was headed before it started a fight with Donald Trump, not making a fuss was putting it out of business.

But the fight with the president of the United States was the best thing that happened to it.

The same is true of many of the greatest advertising campaigns.

Here are just some examples of great fights in advertising (well worth studying): Hertz v Avis, Volkswagen v Detroit, Nike v all sports shoes, Apple v IBM, Virgin v British Airways, Mac v Microsoft, Burger King v McDonald's.

A fight generates interest, which generates free media, which generates more interest.

It encourages people to choose sides, which usually benefits the smaller brand, the one that needs to grow.

The larger brand wants to maintain the status quo, so it wants to keep everything beige, but the smaller brand needs to take market share.

It's all there in Adam Morgan's book *Eating the Big Fish*, that's what challenger brands do, they challenge, they don't run and hide.

And if we don't want to challenge, why are we even advertising?

PART 6

A GREAT IDEA DOESN'T CARE WHO HAS IT

WHY ARE WE ADVERTISING?

When I started in this business all briefs had a section on them headed: WHY ARE WE ADVERTISING?

We don't have this on briefs anymore, it's seen as too obvious to even ask.

"What do you mean 'Why are we advertising?' we want people to buy more of what we make, stupid question."

Well yes and no, of course we want people to buy, but what part does advertising play in making that happen?

That's the real question, before we even start to do any ads.

See my problem is, everyone's got an answer, no one's got a question.

So how do we know we've got the right answer if we don't know what the question is?

And yet that was the original purpose of the planning department, to ask the questions no one else was asking.

To think about the *purpose* of spending money on advertising BEFORE we spent it.

G. K. Chesterton distinguishes between lower-order and higher-order thinking.

He illustrates the difference with a story about an old-fashioned gas streetlight.

A large group of men have gathered round to pull it down.

An old man approaches and says: **"Friends, before we destroy this lamp, let us think about the reason it was built. Let us consider the value of light itself."**

But he's not saying what the mob wants to hear, so they just ignore him.

Then the mob pulls the streetlight over and breaks it into pieces.

Some men wanted to smash it because they wanted the iron.

159

Some men wanted to smash it because they hated the gas company.

Some men thought the light was an intrusion on privacy, some men hated the design.

Some men thought it was old-fashioned. Everyone had a different reason.

So the lamp is destroyed and the different groups argue about their reasons in the dark.

But in the dark they can't see who they're arguing with, and gradually they see maybe the old man had a point, maybe there was a reason for light after all.

But now the lamp is destroyed, and now they don't have any light to discuss it by.

The mob was using lower-order thinking: we know what we want, let's just do it.

The old man was using higher-order thinking: let's investigate the reasons before we act.

Higher-order thinking is superior, but usually avoided because it's more difficult.

This is another expression of a heuristic called Chesterton's Fence.

Someone sees a fence in a field and, seeing no reason for it, decides to tear it down.

Chesterton states that unless you know why the fence was built, you must not tear it down.

You are not capable of addressing a situation until you understand why it exists.

So we should not be advertising until we understand what problem advertising can solve.

How can advertising address a problem without knowing what the problem is?

But it's painfully obvious we don't do this, most of us are just blindly groping around.

Recently I heard some ad professionals discussing another agency's advertising.

They didn't understand the point of an ad, they couldn't remember the brand, they certainly didn't know why anyone would buy the product.

Eventually they ended up at the usual conclusion: **"Well I guess we're talking about it, so it must be working."**

Do we seriously think that is an acceptable answer to: WHY ARE WE ADVERTISING?

Of course not, but we've stopped even asking what the purpose of advertising is.

And when we stop asking questions, we stop thinking.

We just go on autopilot and do our job in the same repetitive, predictable way.

And so, as Geri Seiberling says: **"Marketers have simply become tools of their tools."**

KNOW EVERYONE ELSE'S JOB

In 1965, Jim Clark was in the lead in the British Grand Prix.

He didn't like to save anything for later, he liked to build up as big a lead as he could as fast as he could.

He knew that Formula One cars are subjected to amazing stresses, and after a few dozen laps flat out, things begin to break or wear out.

So he always tried to build up a lead while the car was still in good condition.

Which was just as well because he was 35 seconds ahead, about halfway through the race, when things started to go wrong.

His engine started to leak oil, for a Formula One engine this is bad news.

The reason those cars sound like they're screaming is because the engine is working many times faster than a regular engine.

That means it runs very hot, and the thing lubricating all those spinning parts is the oil.

Without lubrication, the spinning parts overheat and expand and the engine seizes up.

Clark knew this as he watched the oil-pressure gauge drop alarmingly.

But unlike most drivers, Clark knew engines inside-out.

And he noted where the oil-pressure gauge was dropping most was on the corners.

Clark knew engines, he grew up working on tractors on his family's Scottish farm.

He knew if pressure was dropping away on corners, that meant centrifugal force was forcing the oil away from the oil-feed pipe.

So he knew he had to somehow nurse the car round the corners.

And that's where the 35-second lead he'd built up came in handy.

He began slipping the car into neutral on corners, so the engine was merely turning over and didn't need so much oil pressure.

Then he'd slam it back into gear for the straights, where centrifugal force didn't matter and the oil surged back towards the feed pipe.

This cost him time of course, he was losing nearly two seconds a lap and Graham Hill, in his BRM, was closing on him with every lap.

With six laps to go, Clark's lead had been cut to 19 seconds.

With two laps to go, Clark's lead had been cut to 9.6 seconds.

With one lap to go, Clark's lead was down to 6 seconds.

And Clark crossed the finish line just 3.2 seconds ahead of Graham Hill.

With that attention to detail, Clark won the Formula One World Championship that year and the Indianapolis 500.

In its list of the best Formula One drivers, the *Times* rates Clark as the greatest-ever.

Not just because of his driving skill.

But what enabled him to drive that way was he knew every detail of how the car worked.

He didn't just know his own job, he knew everyone else's and that gave him an advantage.

Where another driver would have pulled into the pits, Clark knew he could slip into neutral for the corners because he understood the engine as well as any mechanic.

That's always our secret advantage, to understand the jobs of anyone who impacts on us.

For us it's directors, photographers, typographers, animators, illustrators.

But it's also planners (strategists), and media, and account handlers, and clients.

If we understand their jobs then we are more able to take the decisions that impact on us and our work, rather than leaving it up to them.

I've seen this many times, we often beat people because we looked places they didn't.

They didn't look because they didn't think it was their job.

Well they're right, it isn't their job.

Which is exactly why knowing about it gives you an unfair advantage.

I DON'T KNOW WHAT I WANT, BUT I WANT IT NOW

In 2005, Kyle MacDonald wondered if you could trade a paperclip for a house.

Obviously not, but what if you traded it for something better and kept going, bit by bit?

He decided to see if it was possible, he opened a website called 'The Paperclip Challenge'.

Two girls offered to swap the paperclip for a fish-shaped pen.

Someone saw the pen and offered to swap a hand-sculpted doorknob for it.

Someone saw the doorknob and offered to swap a camp stove for it.

Someone else had just bought a new snowmobile and was willing to swap their old snowmobile for the camp stove.

(Now it was getting interesting – he went from a paperclip to a snowmobile.)

Someone wanted the snowmobile and offered to swap a camping trip in Canada for it.

(People were seeing things they wanted but couldn't afford, so they were thinking what *could* they offer in trade, it was becoming fun.)

Someone wanted the camping trip and offered to swap a large van for it.

A rock group wanted the van so they swapped it for a recording contract.

(This was old-fashioned bartering, you may not have money but you can get creative, what else could you offer?)

A musician offered his apartment, rent-free for a year, for the recording contract.

Alice Cooper's secretary needed somewhere to live, she offered an afternoon with her boss for the rent-free apartment.

Someone then offered a motorised KISS snow globe for the afternoon with Alice Cooper.

Colin Bernstein was a Hollywood producer who collected snow globes, the one he was missing was the motorised KISS snow globe.

He offered a paid-and-credited speaking part in his next movie for the snow globe.

Then the town of Kipling, Saskatchewan, offered a small house for the role in the movie.

They had a population of just 1,000 and had built some houses they wanted to sell.

So they advertised that auditions for the part in the movie would be held in their town.

3,000 people showed up, the whole event took place under a giant red paperclip logo.

The story, and the town of Kipling, got nationwide media exposure.

MacDonald had managed to trade a paperclip for a house, but it had taken him a year and 14 trades, and that's the lesson for us if we want to learn it.

MacDonald swapped something for a slightly better thing, all along the way, bit by bit.

But ad people see the end point and think that's what you do, swap a paperclip for a house.

I've often heard clients say **"We want a campaign like Virgin"** not understanding it took ages to build the Virgin brand, they spent millions upon millions, and had celebrity billionaire Richard Branson as their spokesperson for decades.

So what we *should* be looking for is an idea that can change and evolve in stages over time until it eventually takes us where we want to go.

That used to be called **"an idea with legs"** and the best ad people could recognise one.

For instance, Compare the Market has been changing and evolving their 'meerkats' for 13 years, they now own the market.

Meanwhile, Confused.com and Money Supermarket (who used to own the market) have had many totally new campaigns in the same time.

Meerkats started with a simple idea then kept evolving it in small stages, the other two companies kept trying to do it in one leap and, when that didn't work, started again.

Figuratively speaking, they wanted to swap a paperclip for a house straight away.

But you don't just jump to the top of the ladder, you have to go up a rung at a time.

Evolving a campaign is putting money on top of the pile you've spent ages building.

But a new campaign means starting all over again at the bottom trying to build a new pile.

A decent ad agency should be able to explain the difference to a client.

THINK SMALL

In 1921, Franklin D. Roosevelt contracted polio, he was 39 years old.

He became crippled for life, hardly leaving his wheelchair.

In 1927, he founded the Georgia Warm Springs Foundation to combat polio in children.

But polio was an epidemic and his foundation needed to sound impressive.

So he changed the name to the National Foundation for Infantile Paralysis.

But it sounded pompous and irrelevant, it couldn't raise enough funds.

Roosevelt asked Eddie Cantor, one of the biggest stars of the time, to help.

He asked him if he could get everyone in America to send a dollar towards research.

Cantor said it was the depression, times were tough, nobody had a spare dollar.

Then he joked, maybe he could get everyone to send a dime.

Both men went quiet, then they looked at each other.

A dime was actually more poignant than a dollar, a dime felt more appropriate for helping children, in fact they could ask children for a dime.

They made a cinema commercial, it was due to run before the main feature film.

Usually what ran in that slot was a news roundup called **'The March of Time'**.

They thought they could use that space for their appeal and call it **'The March of Dimes'**.

The public loved it, it felt like thousands of children marching along together to each help in their own little way.

As Eddie Cantor said in the appeal: **"Nearly everyone can send a dime. But it takes only ten dimes to make a dollar and if a million people send only one dime, the total will be $100,000."**

The appeal touched the hearts of ordinary people everywhere.

In the first month, the White House received $268,000 in dimes (around $4.6 million today).

In his birthday radio broadcast, Franklin D. Roosevelt said the following:

"During the past few days, bags of mail have been coming, literally by the truck load, to the White House. Yesterday between forty and fifty thousand letters came to the mail room, today an even greater number. How many I cannot tell you for we can only estimate by counting the stuffed mail bags.

In all the bags are dimes and quarters and even dollar bills – gifts from grown-ups and children – mostly from children who want to help other children get well.

It is glorious to have one's birthday associated with a work like this."

The name **March of Dimes** caught people's imagination so much that they changed the name from National Foundation for Infantile Paralysis to **March of Dimes**.

And it was so successful that it's still the name ninety years later.

Money flowed in at such a rate that it funded Dr. Jonas Salk's work into finding a vaccine, by 1955 March of Dimes had contributed over $2.2 billion.

Just in time too, in 1938 polio cases were 1.3 per thousand children. Between 1943 and 1950 it was up to 10 cases per thousand. Between 1950 and 1956 it doubled to 20 cases per thousand. In one year, 1952, there were 52,000 cases and 3,000 deaths.

But March of Dimes helped fund the vaccine, and by 1962 it dropped to just 1,000 cases.

In 1979, there were no cases at all in the USA.

Since 1988, polio worldwide is down by 99%, and expected to disappear totally.

March of Dimes now funds research into all infant birth defects.

It wasn't pompous, pretentious language that cured polio.

It was talking to people like human beings, like every little bit, every individual, counted.

It made everyone feel they could do something, it made everyone feel important.

It wasn't thinking big, it was thinking small.

REALITY ISN'T PERFECT

Before mobile phones, all calls were made from landlines or phone boxes.

If you didn't have enough money you dialled the operator and, in the UK, asked if you could **'reverse the charges'** or, in the US, asked if you could **'call collect'**.

The operator dialled the number and if they agreed to pay for it, the call went through.

In the US, AT&T had a virtual monopoly, they owned the market.

But in 1993, a company called MCI decided the market-share opportunity was people aged 18–23, young people going away to college.

They'd be calling their parents long-distance and, like all students, wouldn't have money to spend on phone calls.

Their parents would just tell them to reverse the charges (call collect).

But calling collect via AT&T was expensive, because it involved paying an operator to make the connection.

MCI introduced an automatic service, you dialled a prefix then the number and bypassed the operator, so it was cheaper.

The prefix MCI used was 1-800-COLLECT, then your number.

This was so successful that MCI's market share went up from 14% to 20%.

In the same period AT&T's market share fell from 66% to 60%.

So AT&T quickly introduced their own direct-dial collect call service.

They told customers to use the prefix 1-800-OPERATOR, followed by the number.

For me, this is where MCI's real creative brilliance came in.

MCI knew that Americans aren't very good at spelling.

They knew lots of them would remember the word OPERATOR, but spell it OPERATER.

Now, the word itself was simply a mnemonic.

It was actually just a number: 673-72867.

All MCI had to do was buy the number 673-72837 (changing the 6 to a 3 changed 'O' to 'E').

So every time someone mis-spelled OPERATOR as OPERATER, they'd get put through to MCI long-distance instead of AT&T.

It worked brilliantly, every time AT&T advertised their 1-800-OPERATOR prefix, lots of people dialled 1-800-OPERATER and MCI's business went up.

All this time, MCI never mentioned the fact that they'd hijacked AT&T's prefix, they just let AT&T do their advertising for them.

Why not: MCI were spending $150 million, but AT&T were spending $1.4 *billion*.

Eventually AT&T discovered MCI's decoy, and cancelled their 1-800-OPERATOR prefix.

They then had to spend millions more dollars telling customers NOT to use it.

What I love is that MCI never said a word about this, they kept it absolutely quiet.

Because they didn't have their thinking restricted by experts with MBAs who couldn't think any further than what they'd learned from marketing textbooks.

MCI's thinking, and their growth in revenue and share, came from understanding that they'd have to think beyond marketing textbooks.

Their advantage was they weren't restricted by conventional wisdom.

By thinking about the real world with REAL people they were able to leave the competition flat-footed.

AT&T did their job according to the way conventional wisdom said consumers behave.

MCI did their job according to the way real people actually behave.

And you won't learn that from marketing textbooks.

In the real world, there are so many more opportunities for real creative thinking.

THE AVERAGE IS NOT THE MAJORITY

In school, I was told the average life expectancy in the third world was 35 years.

So naturally I thought most people died at 35 years old.

Years later I found this wasn't true.

The biggest cause of death was infant mortality, children dying before age five.

If they grew up, they had every chance of living to 70.

So some died as babies, some died at 70, split the difference and you get 35.

Which is why the average was 35, although most people didn't die at 35.

We tend to confuse the average with the majority.

But the average doesn't exist in the real world, it's just a number on a page.

In 1952, the US Air Force was changing from propeller planes to jets.

Everything happened twice as fast in jets, so a pilot had to react twice as fast.

They began having more and more crashes, 17 in just one day.

They found the pilots couldn't move fast enough to do the things they needed to do at that speed, the problem was the cockpits.

The cockpits were still designed to fit an average size used in 1926, when aircraft were fabric-covered biplanes.

They needed to see if the average size of a pilot had changed in 30 years.

So they got a young Harvard graduate, Gilbert Daniels, to conduct a survey.

He measured 4,063 pilots across 140 size dimensions.

Then he took the top ten dimensions and averaged them out: height, shoulders, chest, waist, hips, legs, reach, torso, neck, thigh.

Then he ran the numbers, he expected most pilots to fit into the overall average.

But he found not one single pilot was average.

Some may be average in one area, but not in others.

Even taking just three dimensions: neck, waist, reach, he found only 3.5% of pilots fitted.

He found there was no such thing as an average pilot.

So now the Air Force had a problem, they couldn't build a cockpit for the average pilot because no such person existed.

In fact, for the first time, Daniels himself realised that average didn't exist anywhere.

He said: **"It was clear to me that if you wanted to design something for an individual human being, the average was completely useless."**

It might be worth thinking about that when we talk about **"the average consumer"**.

It might be worth remembering that they don't exist.

We are marketing and advertising to a fallacy.

How the US Air Force solved the problem was with a motto: BAN THE AVERAGE, DESIGN TO THE EDGES.

But how could they do that, they couldn't design a cockpit for each individual pilot.

No they couldn't, but they could let the individual design their own cockpit.

They came up with something we take for granted today – adjustability.

The seat height, the legroom, the seat angle, the controls, were all made adjustable so the individual could get the cockpit to fit perfectly.

Something we take for granted in cars today.

They adjusted the technology to the individual, not vice versa, and of course it worked.

We may want to think of that, instead of just tapping average demographics into an algorithm and spraying average adverts at people who fit that average.

That non-existent average.

Even Einstein knew the average person doesn't exist.

He said: **"Everyone is a genius, but if you judge a fish by its ability to climb a tree it will spend its life thinking it's stupid."**

STEPPING UP

In the US there are about 25 million physically disabled people.

By 1990, they had decided that inequality made their disability even worse.

They wanted to go onto buses, into shops and restaurants, cinemas, art galleries, they wanted access everywhere normal people have it.

The Americans with Disabilities Act spent ages being debated without getting signed.

There was delay after delay.

Asking and pleading just didn't seem to be working.

So the disabled people did what that the very best advertising does.

Instead of simply talking about it they used a demonstration.

Sixty disabled people on crutches and in wheelchairs went to the Capitol Building in Washington.

That's the seat of US government and it was built with all the grandeur and magnificence the US could muster, five flights of marble steps lead up to the magnificent, commanding entrance.

And 60 disabled people came to the bottom of these steps, then threw away their crutches and fell out of their wheelchairs, and 60 disabled people began to crawl up the Capitol Building steps.

Demonstrating the only way they could access the building.

There are 79 hard, wide marble steps, and the sight of 60 disabled people dragging themselves up those steps couldn't have been more contrasting, or more shaming, to the supposed grandeur of the building.

And, what made it even more touching, as well as the 60 disabled adults dragging their bodies up those steps, there was a ten-year-old girl.

Jennifer Keelan-Chaffins had cerebral palsy, but she dropped from her wheelchair to the ground and began dragging herself up the stairs alongside the grownups.

As she remembered much later, when she asked for water dozens of reporters and cameramen offered her bottles of water.

The sight of disabled people being reduced to crawling up the magnificent steps of the government of the most powerful and prideful nation in the world was one thing.

But a little child scraping her hands and knees bloody on those hard marble steps was even more dramatic.

And to do it outside the very chamber where the Disability Act was being debated made it so much more poignant.

Without saying a word it demonstrated what disabled Americans have to do to get access to the same privilege as ordinary citizens.

It demonstrated what their disability, and their government, had reduced them to.

It showed the power of a simple demonstration over non-stop demand and rhetoric.

Shortly after they dragged their bodies up those steps, the Americans with Disabilities Act was signed into law.

Now every bus, train, plane, restaurant, and shop has to offer disabled access.

The physically disabled have equal access to jobs, eating, travelling, and toilets.

Which is a great lesson about the way the best advertising works.

Not with claims and speeches, and promises, and demands, but with a simple, powerful demonstration of the facts.

Something that everyone can see for themselves, that suddenly brings the truth home.

People don't respond well to lectures.

What works is the facts coming together in their own mind to form an opinion.

BAD DATA

In 2018 the **British Medical Journal** published a paper by Professor Robert Yeh of the Harvard Medical School.

It concerned jumping from aircraft with and without a parachute.

The main finding was that a parachute made no difference to your chances of survival:

"The paper, titled 'Parachute Use to Prevent Death and Major Trauma When Jumping from Aircraft; Randomised Controlled Trial' finds that the safety devices do not significantly reduce the likelihood of death or major injury for people jumping from an aircraft as compared with the control group, equipped only with empty backpacks."

Of the 92 people interviewed for the study, only 23 were found eligible to take part.

Twelve jumped from a plane with a parachute. Thirteen jumped without a parachute.

Findings were that neither group suffered any significant harm or injury. In fact outcomes were identical whether wearing a parachute or not.

But hidden in the middle of the paper was a sentence with a barely noticeable caveat:

"The participants might have been at lower risk of death or major trauma because they jumped from an average altitude of 0.6m (standard deviation 0.1) from an aircraft moving at an average 0 km/h (standard deviation 0)."

In other words, the plane they jumped from was stationery on the ground.

A bit like jumping off a chair.

Which, although it was only included as a caveat in the paper – a mere aside – actually made all the difference.

Without reading that part, everyone automatically assumes the results concern jumping from a plane thousands of feet high moving at hundreds of miles an hour.

Our brains add together the words: 'airplane'–'jump'–'parachute' and supply a picture of someone jumping into a clear blue sky.

This is the reason Professor Robert Yeh wrote the paper.

He wanted to demonstrate the way we leap on details in research papers and sensationalise the sexy parts.

We then run away with the part that makes a great headline without bothering with the mundane part that won't help the story.

The study was a satire on the misuse of research and misunderstanding of data. As he said himself: the context is critical.

I watched TV and read the papers a while back.

The news was full of the fact that research had shown drinking bottle of wine a week increased the risk of cancer.

But that's taken in limbo, with no context.

No one bothered to ask why anyone was drinking a bottle of wine a week.

Maybe it was due to increased stress, maybe stress causes cancer, with or without the wine.

But no one bothered to dig any deeper because they'd found an exciting story.

As the founder of the discipline of mathematical statistics, Karl Pearson, said: **"Correlation does not imply causation."**

As in the parachute example, the wrong question reveals certain data, but ignoring the context can give the wrong answer.

The real question wasn't about the difference between jumping with and without a parachute.

The real question was about the difference between jumping from a stationery object on the ground and a moving object in the air.

But the data can't reveal that, because the data wasn't asked that question.

Data is just numbers, it can't provide conclusions, that's not its job.

Because a human should possess software that data doesn't: common sense.

WHAT'S THE GOAL?

I was reading an article on a philosophy blog about Albert Camus and his time as a goalkeeper.

"There is something appropriate about a philosopher like Camus stationing himself between the sticks. It is a lonely calling, an individual isolated within a team ethic, one who plays to different constraints. If his team scores, the keeper knows it is nothing to do with him. If the opposition score, however, it is all his fault.

Standing sentinel in goal, Camus had plenty of time to reflect on the absurdist nature of his position."

I'd never thought of a goalkeeper like that, a man outside the team.

A man who can lose the game all on his own, and the pressure of knowing that.

It led me to think of Wim Wender's film: *The Goalkeeper's Fear of the Penalty*.

It's about a goalkeeper who has committed a murder and wonders where to hide.

"The goalkeeper attends a football match and witnesses a penalty kick.

The goalkeeper describes what it is like to face a penalty: should he dive to one side, and if he does will the kicker aim for the other?

It is a psychological confrontation in which each tries to outfox the other.

In parallel with this, the goalkeeper, rather than go on the run, returns to his hometown and lives in plain sight. He doesn't know if the police are looking for him in particular, but the police are not necessarily looking for someone who isn't trying to hide."

Which again made me think how lonely it is to be a goalkeeper, especially the pressure when facing penalties.

I recently read some statistics about 965 penalties taken across 10 seasons.

168 had been saved, that's 17.4%, by goalkeepers who had dived to the left or to the right.

But the most surprising statistic showed that if they hadn't dived, simply stayed in the middle of the goal, they would have saved 33% of the penalties.

So the question is, why didn't they just stand still and double the number of saves?

This is what Daniel Kahneman calls **'norm theory'**, he describes it as **'broken emotions'**.

And it's dictated by what the crowd wants to see.

Basically, if we perform to the expected norm, and it works, we get greater appreciation.

If we go against the norm, and it fails, we get greater disappointment.

So the safest route is to perform as the crowd expects: if we succeed it's great and even if we fail, it's not too bad.

The norm for a goalkeeper would be making spectacular dives, not standing still.

Crowds don't do statistics, they'd rather see a goalkeeper diving across the goal than just standing still.

I once asked a professional goalkeeper what he thought of West Ham's goalie.

He said he didn't think he was very good.

I said, **"How can you say that, he's made some spectacular saves?"**

The professional said, **"That's how you know he's not very good, you only make spectacular saves when you're out of position.**

If you've got good positional sense, you are where the ball is going to come.

It doesn't look so impressive to the crowd, but you let in less goals and win more matches that way."

And that always seemed a good parallel for what we do.

We play to the crowd by doing work just to impress our peers, or win awards.

We're not interested in statistics of what works, just how we look to the crowd.

Do we get the best write-ups in the trade press, are we fashionable?

We may not get the best results, but we make some spectacular moves and look impressive.

Because we're out of position and playing to the crowd.

USING CUSTOMERS AS ADVERTS

Recently, my daughter, Jade, and I were walking down West End Lane.

It's a busy street in south Hampstead and there are two bookshops near each other.

One was open but empty, it didn't look particularly inviting so we just walked past.

But the next one had a wooden sandwich board outside, with 20 little brown parcels tied with string stuck onto it.

At the top was written: **"Blind Date with a Book – £6.99"**.

Then, on each little package was written a brief synopsis, without telling you which book was inside.

One said: **"Righting wrongs – The list – Marriage – Disabled child – Laugh out loud."**

The next one said: **"Jailbird – 18th Century – Erotic – Ghosts – Magical Realism."**

A third said: **"Odd family – Yorkshire – Newly divorced – Romantic comedy – Cute and charming."**

Another one said: **"Escape plan – Bossy husband – Rediscovery – New beginnings – Provence."**

Yet another one said: **"Good vs Evil – Fears and desires – Fantasy horror – Classic – Ride the carnival."**

And Jade and I started to read them out loud and see if we could guess which book was being described.

Jade read one aloud that said: **"Left to die – Mountaineering – Winter horror – Historical – Chills."**

She said: **"That's got to be *Touching the Void* by Joe Simpson, that's my favourite."**

I read one aloud that said: **"Replicants – Dystopian earth – Bounty hunter – SF masterpiece – Ingenious."**

I said: **"I bet that's *Do Androids Dream of Electric Sheep?* The book that Ridley Scott got the idea for *Blade Runner* from."**

And people saw us talking and began reading the words on the little brown packages on the other side of the sandwich board.

Pretty soon there were half-a-dozen of us around the display, reading the descriptions.

Some of us began to go inside to look at the bookshelves, some other people saw us reading and chatting and also went inside.

The interesting thing for me was that during all this time, no one went into the other bookshop.

That bookshop just expected you to walk in, but this bookshop was smarter, they did it creatively.

First they didn't mention going inside, they just stopped you with a funny line: **"Blind Date with a Book – £6.99".**

Then they intrigued you with tantalising descriptions which, if you were a book lover, you'd have to stop and read.

And all the while having you act as an advertisement for their shop by making it look busy and fun, the sort of place book lovers went as opposed to the other empty shop.

The point was, two bookshops near each other, one made an effort and one didn't.

One owner made their bookshop more appetising, more appealing, and they did it without anyone even noticing that's what they were doing.

No online advertising, no targeting, no algorithms, no big data, just a little bit of creativity. You love books, we love books, let's have a bit of fun with it.

The job of the advertising wasn't to sell you something as you walked by.

The job was to stop you, intrigue you, and seduce you into the shop.

I think we could all learn a lot about how advertising, marketing, and media work from that little bookshop in West End Lane.

As Adam Barratt said: **"Don't try to lead a horse to water – try to make it thirsty."**

PART 7

HOW TO PUT IDEAS INTO WORDS

WORDS BEAT DATA

In 1842, the Second Report of the Children's Employment Commission was released.

Young girls were spending 16 hours a day, six days a week, sewing garments.

Boys as young as eight were pulling coal carts in the mines, 11 hours a day.

Children were losing their limbs, sometimes their lives, cleaning huge machinery.

The choice was simple, work in inhuman conditions or starve to death.

Not that those facts bothered everyone.

The Reverend Thomas Malthus saw no need to worry about the poor.

He said: **"Better to let the poor starve naturally and decrease the surplus population."**

That was the attitude of the majority of the wealthy.

The poor were stupid and lazy, they had no use but physical labour.

There was no more point educating them than educating a horse or an ox.

The wealthy believed that a rich man was a self-made man.

Consequently the pursuit of wealth for its own sake was a worthy goal.

A member of the commission asked a young writer to help with a pamphlet to turn public opinion against the cruel treatment of the poor.

To bring the greed of the wealthy to everyone's attention.

The young writer's name was Charles Dickens, and the pamphlet was to be called: **'An Appeal to the People of England on behalf of the Poor Man's Child'**.

Dickens visited tin mines in Cornwall, and Field Lane Ragged School in London's East End.

What he saw there made him too angry to write a pamphlet.

Reason alone wouldn't change anything.

Someone else could do facts and figures, he needed to move people emotionally.

He said to the head of the commission, Dr Southwood Smith: **"You will certainly feel that a sledge-hammer has come down with twenty times the force of the first idea."**

And Charles Dickens wrote A Christmas Carol.

He had seen a Scottish grave inscribed, **"Ebenezer Lennox Scroggie – a meal man"**.

A meal man was a corn merchant, but Dickens misread it as **"a mean man"**.

That became his main character, Ebenezer Scrooge, a man who loves money above all else.

A man blind to the suffering and misery it causes, and the terrible waste of humanity.

A ghost visits Scrooge and shows him various scenes: past, present, and future.

Scrooge is touched by the plight of a little crippled boy called Tiny Tim.

When Scrooge asks the ghost if the boy will live, the ghost answers: **"Better to let the poor die naturally and decrease the surplus population."**

The exact words of the Reverend Thomas Malthus.

He shows Scrooge two starved children, just like Dickens saw in the ragged school.

He tells Scrooge: **"The boy is Ignorance, the girl is Want. Beware them both but most of all beware the boy."**

Eventually, having learned the message in the dreams, Scrooge changes his ways.

The message being that employers are responsible for the well-being of their workers, something that never even occurred to the wealthy before.

For the first time social responsibility was expressed in emotional, human terms instead of dry facts and cold figures and data.

In the first year, the book had to be reprinted 13 times; in the US alone it eventually sold 2 million copies.

People who would never read a dry, factual report read the book again and again.

Over the years, it's been adapted 48 times for plays, 28 times for films, 87 times for TV, 25 times for radio, four times for opera, twice for ballet, 15 times for graphic novels, and twice for video games.

Since it was written, Dickens' book has been taught in schools every year at Christmas.

As Walt Disney said: **"We have to entertain in order to educate, because the other way round doesn't work."**

WRITE LIKE PEOPLE TALK

The Texas Department of Transportation (TxDOT) had a problem.

It was costing them $20 million a year to clean up litter left on their highways.

Every year they ran ad campaigns saying things like: **"Keep America Beautiful"** and **"Stop Litter in Texas"** but these did nothing.

And the problem was increasing 17% year on year.

The commissioner, John Austin, asked ad agency, GSD&M, for help.

GSD&M's Tim McClure asked researcher Daniel B. Syrek to define the problem for them.

He said most of the highway litter came from young men aged 18–24.

Cruising around in their pickups throwing beer cans and fast food trash out the window.

They were young and rebellious and the litter was someone else's problem.

And McClure realised the current ads just weren't talking these people's language.

These young men didn't connect with littering or keeping America beautiful.

He had to talk to them in their own language.

And he remembered, when he was a child, his mum would say: **"This room is a mess"** or **"Clear up this mess"** or **"Whose mess is this?"**

And he thought, that's it – that's the language people use.

And so he wrote **"Don't Mess With Texas"**.

It was not only the right language, it was the right attitude: cocky and challenging.

But getting the board of the TxDOT to see that was another matter.

McClure says: **"They were all about 107 years old. One member said to us 'Can't you at least say "Please"?' And I said no, that would ruin it."**

Eventually, Don Clark, director of Travel and Information, overruled the board and ran it.

To get it into the language, they began giving away bumper stickers in truck stops and diners the target market used.

Then the next year, the TV campaign launched.

During the 50th annual Cotton Bowl, Stevie Ray Vaughan picked out a blues track on his guitar while the VO said: **"Each year we spend over $20 million picking up trash along our Texas highways. Messing with Texas isn't just an insult to the Lone Star State, it's a crime."**

Then Stevie Ray Vaughan looked at camera and said **"Don't mess with Texas"**.

Suddenly everyone wanted that line on badges, t-shirts, hats, bumper stickers.

And every famous Texan wanted to be seen in an ad with that line.

Over the next 12 years they made 26 TV commercials with people who were proud to be Texans, like: Willie Nelson, Matthew McConaughey, George Foreman, Chuck Norris, LeAnn Rimes, George Strait, Asleep at the Wheel, The Fabulous Thunderbirds.

Even the future president of the United States, George W. Bush, used it in a speech.

So how did talking to people in their own language work as an ad campaign?

In the first year the campaign ran there was a 29% decrease in litter.

In the second year there was a 54% decrease in litter.

And by the third year there was a 72% decrease in litter.

All by talking to people in the language they used, instead of the language the board of the TxDOT thought they should use.

By talking *to* people instead of talking *at* people.

Suddenly people could identify with it and were proud and happy to use it.

That's how you get a campaign to go viral, it doesn't take money, it takes brains.

And it takes a willingness to get inside your audience's heads and speak like they do.

In a way that makes sense to them, instead of sounding like a lecture.

That's how you get them to do what you want.

By understanding what they want.

KNOWLEDGE NEGLECT

In 1970, two US psychologists, Gregory Kimble and Lawrence Perlmutter, wrote an article for the *Psychological Review*.

It showed the responses of people to a question, when the first four answers are filled in and the fifth is left blank:

Q 1) What tree do acorns come from?

A) Oak.

Q 2) What do we call a funny story?

A) Joke.

Q 3) What sound does a frog make?

A) Croak.

Q 4) What's another name for a cape?

A) Cloak.

Q 5) What's the white of an egg called?

A) Yolk.

Now after a few seconds thought we can see the last answer is wrong.

But the immediate answer given by respondents fell in line with what they thought was expected.

The mind had built up a rhythm and an expected an 'oke' sound.

This is known as the 'Yolk Phenomenon'.

In 1981, two other US psychologists, Thomas Erikson and Mark Mattson, wrote an article for the *Journal of Verbal Learning and Verbal Behaviour*.

It concerned the answers a group of respondents gave to the question: **"How many animals of each kind did Moses take into the Ark?"**

As we might expect, most respondents answered two.

But the correct answer isn't two, the correct answer is none.

Moses didn't take any animals into the Ark, Noah did.

This became known as the 'Moses Illusion' and, like the Yolk Phenomenon, is an example of what is known as 'Knowledge Neglect'.

Knowledge Neglect is a phenomenon whereby we actually know the correct answer, but are distracted by something else in the question.

In the case of the Moses Illusion, respondents were distracted by the part of the question: **'how many animals?'**

They answered that part and ignored the flaw in the question itself.

Which made them give an incorrect answer.

This is what we do in advertising, we answer the trivial part and ignore the vital part.

Common sense says that no advertising can work unless it's noticed.

Common sense says that no advertising can work unless it's remembered.

Common sense says no advertising can work unless there's a reason to act.

But all these are ignored because we have entire departments focussed on nothing but brand purpose.

So advertising is run purely to illustrate brand purpose.

Getting noticed is ignored, getting remembered is ignored, a reason to act is ignored.

They are taken for granted just like the rhyme for yolk or the name Moses.

Advertising is a prime example of Knowledge Neglect.

We are the people who read the publications where these articles are published, yet we behave exactly the same as the people described.

We've forgotten the purpose of advertising is: get noticed, remembered, and acted upon.

Not merely as a container for a banal brand purpose.

THE BANKSY OF GRAMMAR

In Bristol, there's a man who hates bad punctuation.

Lots of us do, the difference is this man is doing something about it.

For over a decade, he's been travelling the streets at night correcting punctuation on signs.

He finds the incorrect use of apostrophes particularly annoying.

So at night, he takes out his ten-foot pole and sticky-backed plastic, and either adds or removes apostrophes as necessary.

One of his first corrections was **Amys Nail's**: no apostrophe where it should be in **Amy's**, and an apostrophe where it shouldn't be in **Nails**.

Next was **Cambridge Motor's**, apostrophe successfully removed.

Then at Tesco: **Fish is not just for Friday's**, apostrophe successfully removed.

Gardeners Patch and **Roxfords Pet Shop**, both had apostrophes added.

As did **Vincenzo & Sons Gentlemens Hair Stylist**, and **Herberts Bakery**.

Computer Course's, had the apostrophe removed, as did **Pizza Fast Fire'd**.

Please Clean Up After You're Dogs, had the apostrophe and the letter e removed.

Authenticity at it's Best, also had the apostrophe removed.

Toilet ONLY for Disabled Elderly Pregnant Children had to have several commas added.

Tux & Tail Gentlemens Outfitters needed an apostrophe, as did **Robin Hoods of Treece**.

He calls himself a grammar vigilante.

Normally I'd find someone like this petty and pedantic, but here I have some sympathy.

I'm all for breaking the rules when there's a reason.

What I don't agree with is sloppiness and laziness.

These rules hadn't been broken, they'd been ignored by people who couldn't be bothered.

The purpose of a sign is communication.

That means it must be correct for the person making the communication and the person receiving it, otherwise it's not communicating.

For many years, I worked with one of London's best art directors, Gordon Smith.

Gordon was dyslexic so he had a legitimate excuse for bad spelling if he wanted.

But Gordon was too proud for that, he always carried a small electronic speller in his pocket and checked absolutely every word, every comma and apostrophe.

No one was going to do his job for him.

Gordon paid attention to every little detail that went into HIS ads.

Which of course is the attitude that made him one of London's best art directors, instead of just another sloppy, lazy also-ran.

Bad spelling is fine where it's appropriate, like text messaging.

There, everyone knows that's the way you communicate, everyone expects it: writing ur instead of your, and coz instead of because saves time, so fair enough.

But to transfer that thinking to something that takes weeks to put together is just a pose: let me prove how young and trendy I am: **"Down wiv da kidz"**.

It's like your granny in hot pants, unless there's a genuine reason for it.

In a Conservative election poster, Saatchi's once wrote: EDUKASHUN ISN'T WORKING.

Fair enough, that was mis-spelled for a reason, it wouldn't have been nearly so good as: EDUCATION ISN'T WORKING.

But whoever wrote those Bristol signs wasn't trying to be clever, they just couldn't be arsed.

They weren't trying to break rules, they just didn't care what anyone thought.

They didn't give a damn for the details.

Which to my mind shows a level of contempt for our audience.

"It's near enough, it'll do."

Who cares anyway?

Well, if we can't be bothered, why should anyone else be bothered with it?

SIMPLICITY WORKS, COMPLEXITY DOESN'T

By 1830, people began wondering if electricity could be used to communicate over long distances.

It would be called telegraphy, and there were two competing versions.

In the UK there was Sir William Cooke and Sir Charles Wheatstone's; in the US there was Leonard Gale and Samuel Morse's.

Cooke and Wheatstone's system was the more elaborate, it sent electric signals that would move needles at the receiving end into semaphore-like patterns.

It required complicated equipment to send and receive, and also two people – one to watch the needles and one to write down the letters as they were shouted out.

It worked well enough in the UK, where it was mainly between cities.

But Gale and Morse's system was better suited to the vast open spaces and small towns of America.

Their system was much simpler, it just switched the electric current on or off, it could be on very briefly or slightly longer, that was it.

If it was short it counted as a dot, slightly longer and it counted as a dash.

They arranged the dots and dashes into an alphabet, and that was all there was to it, no moving parts, no elaborate equipment.

The simple sound of the dots and dashes meant it only took one operator to write down the letters without having to look at the machine.

The letter E would be just one dot, the letter I would be two dots, the letter T just one dash, the letter M two dashes, the other letters a mixture of dots and dashes.

One man sitting on his own in the middle of nowhere could send and receive messages.

The simple code was called Morse, named after the inventor.

Cooke and Wheatstone's system disappeared, Morse Code dominated all communication for the next hundred years.

Cooke and Wheatstone's failed because it depended on complicated *hardware*, the Morse version succeeded because it depended on the simplest possible *software*, people.

Morse Code could be learnt and used anywhere, with or without electricity.

Ships at sea could use lights to blink messages in dots and dashes, prisoners in jail could tap messages on the bars using tin cups.

The system adapted to people, even without any hardware at all.

In a PoW camp in 1941, Major Alexis Casdagli knitted a wall hanging which he took with him from camp to camp.

The Germans let him display it as an example of how effete the British soldiers were.

But all the other British prisoners could read the pattern that was stitched into it.

Meanwhile, it clearly read: **"FUCK HITLER"** stitched many times over in Morse Code.

In Vietnam in 1966 a downed US pilot was forced to make a video.

To camera, he said: "I get adequate food and clothing and medical care when I require it."

Meanwhile, his eyelids blinked: **"T-O-R-T-U-R-E"** in Morse code.

The reason Morse Code is still in use nearly 200 years after its invention is its simplicity.

Morse knew that, with the human mind, simplicity works and complexity doesn't.

We could learn from that.

Complexity is a security blanket, it makes us feel safer, as if we've been clever.

But actually complexity is weakness, it just means we haven't thought long enough to get to the simple answer.

It means we stopped while it was still complicated, we didn't persevere to simplicity.

So we never bought a ticket into the mind of people.

And that's the place where simplicity always beats complexity.

NO ONE READS THE SMALL PRINT

No one reads the small print, so you can hide anything in there.

The *Guardian* reported how Manchester-based company, Purple, made the point.

In 2017, 22,000 people signed up for free Wi-Fi and, without reading the small print, agreed to 1,000 hours of community service including cleaning toilets and unblocking sewers.

In a previous example, six people agreed to give away their first-born child for eternity, by not reading the small print.

Some companies have fun with it. On 1 April 2010, Gamestation small print stated that unless you unchecked the box, you agreed to **"a non-transferable option to a claim, for now and ever more, on your immortal soul."**

In the Apple iTunes end-user agreement it states: **"We won't be held liable for any delays or failure in performance from any cause beyond our control, including fires, earthquakes, nuclear accidents, and zombie apocalypse."**

So the small print has become a bit of a joke.

No one can seriously be expected to read it, so they scroll past it and tick the box.

Which is exactly what some companies want you to do.

Take travel insurance for instance, Bonnie Solberg was on holiday in Dakota with her husband when he died.

She'd taken out travel insurance beforehand, to cover eventualities like medical expenses, but she hadn't read the small print.

The maximum amount she could reclaim on the policy was $846, so she had to find the remaining $28,333 herself.

Nancy Morgan also took out travel insurance, a policy labelled 'Cancel for Any Reason'.

But again, she didn't read the small print.

When she needed to cancel she found that the reason she gave wasn't one of the reasons listed in the small print, consequently she couldn't get a refund.

This is the sort of behaviour that gives travel insurance companies a bad reputation.

Which is just what travel insurance comparison company Squaremouth didn't want.

So they decided to separate themselves off from everyone else by encouraging their customers to read the small print carefully.

That way there wouldn't be any nasty surprises when it came time to claim.

Squaremouth rewrote the small print on their policy knowing that just 1% would read it.

It was at the bottom of page seven, a line that said: **'It pays to read'** and a short explanation that the first person to notice it would get $10,000.

Donna Andrews was the first person to read Squaremouth's small print.

She was a high school teacher from Georgia who'd majored in consumer economics.

She said, **"I know I sound like a nerd but I learned to read contracts so I don't get taken advantage of."**

She not only won Squaremouth's $10,000 for herself, but another $10,000 for a children's literacy charity, and $5,000 each for the libraries of the schools she teaches at.

Meanwhile, Squaremouth's story was picked up by CBS News, the *Washington Post*, *USA Today*, *Money* magazine, *Forbes* magazine, *Travel + Leisure*, *People* magazine, Yahoo, and *Travel Weekly*.

It generated media coverage way in excess of the $10,000 prize money.

So guess which travel insurance comparison company now has a brand image for trust and honesty.

Imagine how much word of mouth that generated amongst people about to go on holiday and book travel insurance.

Brand is another word for image which is another word for reputation.

And that's a lesson in how you build a brand.

You take the truth and deliver it in a surprising, creative way.

RULE OF THUMB

Since the Middle Ages, common law decreed a woman was her husband's property.

Like anything he owned, animals or children, he had to discipline her from time to time.

Although, he must use reasonable force and not kill her.

In 1782, Judge Francis Buller was required to sit in judgement on such a case.

He referred to an earlier precedent, where a man had been found guilty of beating his wife to death with a pestle (a heavy, club-like kitchen tool).

At the time, the judgement was: **"Though a husband by law may correct his wife, the pestle is no instrument for correction."**

Judge Buller felt the guidelines needed to be more specific, so he ruled: **"A husband may thrash his wife with impunity provided he uses a stick no bigger than his thumb."**

Subsequently the cartoonist, James Gillray, caricatured him as "Judge Thumb".

But the rule persisted, in 1824 in Mississippi a court ruling stated a man was entitled to enforce domestic discipline providing he used a cane no wider than his thumb.

In North Carolina, in 1868, a defendant was found to have used a cane on his wife **"about the thickness of his finger"**.

He was allowed to go free because a finger was thinner than a thumb.

That judgement was later upheld by the Supreme Court.

In 1917, legal scholar Beirne Stedman cited the old common law rule allowing a husband to use: **"moderate personal chastisement on his wife"** so long as the rod was no larger than his thumb.

In 1976, this law was used to illustrate the cliché by women's-rights advocate Del Martin: **"The common law doctrine was modified to allow a husband to whip his wife provided he use something no bigger than his thumb – a rule of thumb, so to speak."**

In 1977, a book on battered women mentioned: "The reason nineteenth century British wives were dealt with so harshly by their husbands and their legal system was the 'rule of thumb'."

Which is how, we are told, the phrase 'rule of thumb' passed into common usage.

Wikipedia defines rule of thumb as: **"An easily learned and easily applied procedure or standard, based on practical experience rather than theory."**

Interestingly, Wikipedia later uses 'rule of thumb' to define heuristics.

"A heuristic is a mental shortcut that allows people to solve problems and make judgements quickly and efficiently. These 'rules of thumb' strategies shorten decision-making time and allow people to function without constantly stopping to think about the next course of action."

In behavioural economics, heuristics are referred to as cognitive biases.

Cognitive is defined as: **"Involving conscious intellectual capacity such as thinking or reasoning."**

Bias is defined as: **"To feel inclination for or against someone or something."**

So, cutting through all the long words, rule of thumb means heuristic, which means prejudiced thinking.

In behavioural economics, cognitive biases include: confirmation bias, availability bias, sunk-cost bias, anchoring bias, framing-effect bias, actor-observer bias, and many more.

And of course, all these are designed to sound intimidating to outsiders.

But remember, they are all actually just common sense dressed up in long words.

They all come back to the rule of thumb.

And the rule of thumb goes back to a silly medieval law.

So don't be frightened by long words, just unpack them and find out what they're actually disguising.

It's a good rule of thumb, or heuristic, to say: **"Excuse me, what does that mean?"**

You'll be surprised how often the people using the long words don't actually know what they mean, or where they came from.

DON'T BE A SCUNTHORPE

A few years back, Scunthorpe Hospital installed a new computer system.

On the first day it was switched on, the staff began using email as usual.

Around lunchtime they noticed they weren't getting any replies to any of their emails.

They quickly checked the new system and found it was working fine, too well in fact.

The problem was the new system's profanity filter, it was geared to spot obscene words and block them.

Of course, a computer system doesn't understand what words are, the only way it can spot words is by connecting a string of letters.

The system had been given a list of seven words which were considered obscene and not to be allowed.

The most obscene of these words was the second, third, fourth, and fifth letters of Scunthorpe's name.

The name that was on every email the staff sent out.

So as soon as anyone outside the hospital pressed reply, the system read the letters on the address and the email was automatically blocked as obscene.

This has become known in computer circles as **'the Scunthorpe problem'**.

Systems all over the world were, and still are, rejecting strings of letters they believe to be offensive words.

Belgian political candidate, Luc Anus, was blocked for this reason.

So was Jeff Gold's website, Shitake Mushrooms.

Arun Dikshit had the same problem, so did Ben Schmuck, also Mike Dickman, Craig Cockburn, Douglas Kuntz, James Butts, and Brian Wankum.

Places like Penistone, Middlesex, Clitheroe, and Lightwater were rejected for the same reason.

The Royal Society for the Protection of Birds was blocked for tits, cocks, boobies and shags.

Manchester Council planning department had problems with emails mentioning erections.

A councillor from Dudley was blocked for telling visitors the local faggots were tasty.

Even Arsenal football club and French TV station Canal Plus had similar problems.

Another filter automatically changed the word ass to butt, so **'classic'** became **'clbuttic'** and **'assassinate'** became **'buttbuttinate'**.

The Horniman Museum faced restrictions, as did several Dick Whittington pantomimes.

So, it would seem the problem with technology is merely excessive vigilance.

Well not quite. American tech writer, Kaveh Wadell, tried an experiment.

He sent seven advertisements to run on Facebook, all contained extremely dangerous, fake Coronavirus advice.

The ads were for a fictitious advertiser called the Self-Preservation Society.

One ad said: "Coronavirus is just a hoax, carry on living your life as normal."

Another ad said: "Social distancing is ineffective, ignore it."

A third said: "People under 30 are completely safe from Coronavirus."

A fourth said: "Don't stay in, just return to normal."

All these ads were approved to run within minutes.

But before they could run, Wadell had the site taken down, he'd made his point.

Facebook made $30 billion from advertising last year, they say they don't have enough human workers, so automated ad-screening is done by algorithms.

But it seems technology is failing on both counts.

It's failing to block what it should block, and blocking what it shouldn't block.

Don't we just need a few good old-fashioned human brains in there somewhere?

Something smarter than technology.

TRUTH IN ADVERTISING?

Thomas Jefferson was one of the founders of the USA, he wrote the Declaration of Independence.

He was a philosopher, in the days when that meant thinking for yourself, and questioning accepted wisdom, which is why he was a revolutionary.

He was opposed to anything he saw as rules laid down to manipulate the gullible.

Which is why he took a razor blade to the Bible and created his own version.

From Matthew, Mark, Luke, and John he cut out everything except Jesus's words.

All the miracles, which were only there to impress, were cut out.

Historian Edwin Scott Gausted explains: **"If a moral lesson was embedded in a miracle, the lesson survived, but the miracle did not. Jefferson maintained Jesus's role as a great moral teacher, not as a shaman or faith healer."**

Jefferson felt Jesus's words had been lost in a show of miracles and magic, put there to dazzle the uneducated and maintain the church's power.

Jefferson himself explained it this way: **"In extracting the pure principles which Jesus taught, we have to strip off the artificial vestments in which they have been muffled by priests, who have travestied them into various forms, as instruments of riches and power to themselves. We must reduce it to the very words only of Jesus, paring off the ambiguity into which they have been led, by giving their own misconceptions and expressing unintelligibly for others what they had not understood themselves. I have performed this operation by cutting verse by verse out of the printed book, and arranging the matter which is evidently his, and which is as easily distinguishable as diamonds in a dunghill."**

When Jefferson had finished, he wrote: **"A more beautiful or precious morsel of ethics I have never seen; it is a document in proof that I am a real Christian, that is to say, a disciple of the doctrines of Jesus."**

Jefferson was a true believer in Christ's words, not just impressed by a superbeing who could perform miracles, he thought that was unnecessary showmanship.

The truth that was so powerful it needed no dressing-up.

But priests were people who didn't see the truth as sufficient, the truth needed to be made attractive for ordinary people, in fact the truth itself was almost irrelevant.

This is often the position when people are convinced that truth isn't enough.

They need to find something more interesting, more persuasive, more compelling.

This is how it is with marketing, they believe the truth alone isn't nearly enough.

In fact, this is the basis for the existence of marketing, that products need an industry of people to go beyond truth, to entice and convince.

Like everyone else, this is what I thought advertising was based on.

When I was a young copywriter at BMP, I was given the launch of a car.

I tried to see how I could sell it, how could I persuade people to buy it?

Eventually I went to see David Batterby, the managing director, I told him I couldn't find any way to sell this car.

David said: **"Look, the people who made this car didn't think 'We'll build it and then find out if an advertising agency can sell it'. They invested millions of pounds in retooling the entire factory to make this car. They didn't do that unless they knew there was a market ready for it. So who did they think would buy it and why?"**

He made me realise there was a truth before any ad agency got involved, there was a truth in the product.

Nowadays *product* is a dirty word, in fact products don't exist, only *brands* exist.

Marketing, especially 'strategists', turn up their nose at the mention of the word *product*.

They need to invent a brand purpose or no one will buy our *brand*.

And yet, strangely enough, people do still buy products, if we can get out of the way.

If we can find the truth.

PART 8

ACCIDENTS, MISTAKES, OR IDEAS?

EVERYTHING HAS VALUE IF YOU LOOK

My mum and dad never agreed on the best way to make a cup of tea.

Mum always put the milk in first, Dad always put the milk in second.

My art director, Gordon Smith, and I had the same problem.

Gordon insisted on putting the milk in first. I say it makes more sense to put it in second.

My wife agrees with Gordon, but George Orwell is on my side, he wrote a famous article about why milk should go in second.

Ronald Fisher was a mathematician working at Rothamsted Experimental Station in Hertfordshire, in 1920.

He offered to make his colleague, biologist Muriel Bristol, a cup of tea.

She watched him make it and said: **"Stop."**

Fisher asked what the problem was.

She said: **"You're putting the milk in first, I don't like it that way."**

Fisher said she was being ridiculous: it's a matter of simple thermodynamics: liquid A added to liquid B is exactly the same as adding liquid B to liquid A, the order is irrelevant.

She insisted it wasn't and she could taste the difference.

As they were both scientists there was only one logical way to test her assertion.

Scientists gathered round as Fisher made eight cups of tea, identical in every way except one.

In four of the cups the milk was added first, in the other four it was added second.

As a blind test, Muriel Bristol had no way of knowing which was which.

But everyone watched as, one after the other, she identified immediately from taste alone which cup of tea was which.

And she was correct eight times out of eight.

Her point was proved, but Fisher wasn't convinced and it bothered him.

Logically it made no sense, as a mathematician there must be a formula for it.

There was truth in numbers, so he began to devise equations.

What was the chance of pure luck? What was the possibility of mistakes? What if he used a larger sample size? What if he added random variations?

Without realising it, he had moved on from simply analysing a tea test into devising the correct way to run tests to arrive at a more accurate statistical analysis.

And Fisher didn't realise he was inventing the null hypothesis which became the bedrock of the science of statistical analysis.

In 1925 he published **Statistical Methods for Research Workers** which is still the foundation work on statistics taught in universities today.

Anders Hald called Fisher: **"A genius who almost singlehandedly created the foundations for modern statistical science."**

Richard Dawkins called him: **"The greatest biologist since Darwin."**

I don't understand a word about the science of statistics or anything Fisher's written.

But I do know that inspiration will come from the unlikeliest places, even making a cup of tea, so we should look where we don't expect it to be.

George Lucas didn't think he was founding a multi-billion-dollar empire when he began making a science fiction B movie.

Andy Warhol didn't think he was creating an art movement when he silk-screened the soup that was all he could afford to eat.

Steve Jobs didn't think he was revolutionising computers when he bunked into typography classes without paying.

Quentin Tarantino didn't think he was changing cinema when he was working in a video store watching bad foreign films.

You never know where an idea is coming from, because ideas are new combinations.

And it's no good looking in lectures or books or art galleries for inspiration.

They are just places where the creativity has been pre-digested for you to look at.

ACCIDENTAL CREATIVITY

In 1903, Edouard Benedictus was working in his laboratory, he needed a glass jar from the top shelf so he climbed the ladder.

On the way up he knocked off a glass jar from a shelf, it hit the floor and broke.

But the strange thing was, the glass jar held its shape.

Although it was broken, the pieces stayed in the shape of the jar.

Benedictus's assistant had used the glass the previous day, but he hadn't cleaned it.

The inside was coated with the residue of the mixture: cellulose nitrate, or liquid plastic.

It evaporated and coated the glass in a transparent film no one could see.

Benedictus had been reading in a newspaper about the new invention of motor cars.

People were dying in car crashes when they went through the windshield and the glass shards sliced their heads off.

In 1909, Benedictus patented his discovery as safety glass.

But no one was interested until World War One, when the army began using his glass as eyepieces for gasmasks.

Henry Ford saw the possibility and by 1929 safety glass was a standard feature on every Ford car made.

Today, every car made anywhere in the world features Benedictus's accidental discovery.

In 1879, at John Hopkins University, Constantine Fahlberg was experimenting with a coal-tar derivative, benzoic sulfimide.

Like Benedictus's assistant he was lazy, he forgot to wash his hands.

That evening at dinner he ate a bread roll.

The roll was amazingly sweet although it had nothing on it, not even butter.

Fahlberg couldn't work it out until he licked his fingers.

Then he tasted the sweetness and it was obvious, it was the benzoic sulfimide he'd been working with that day.

In 1886 Fahlberg patented it, but again there was no interest until World War One, when it was used as a substitute for sugar, which was in short supply.

That was the main use for it until the 1950s when, for the first time in history, it became fashionable for ordinary people to lose weight.

Fahlberg's accident was known as saccharin, the foundation for the entire dieting industry.

In 1946, Percy Spencer was an engineer at Raytheon working on military applications for the radar magnetron.

While he was experimenting, he felt a gooey mess in his pocket, the chocolate bar he had in there had melted.

The radar magnetron had been producing microwaves, and they heated the chocolate.

Spencer had accidentally invented the microwave oven.

In 1955 it was launched as Radarange, it weighed hundreds of pounds and was a flop.

In 1967, a smaller version was launched, food was packaged to be microwaved and in five years there were a million in use. Today Spencer's accident is in 90% of American homes.

So, accidents can be creative, but what use is that to us?

John Webster always said you have to be open to fortunate accidents along the way.

He told me: **"Your problem is, your ad's as good as it's ever going to get at script stage, you don't leave any room for lucky accidents."**

He was right, I get locked-off into delivering exactly what I've written down.

Fair enough, I'm a copywriter, logic and communication is my job.

But John was an art director, and he saw his job as sprinkling stardust on the logic.

John always looked at accidents for what they added to the idea.

A mis-briefed voice-over, unexpected music, the wrong location, a casting mistake.

Something unexpected that took the idea in a whole new direction.

John's way of thinking reminds me of what Orson Wells said: **"Don't give them what they want. Give them what they never dreamed was possible."**

SWITCHING OFF OUR COMMON SENSE

In 2015, in Chicago, Iftikhar Hussain loaded up his Nissan Sentra.

He and his wife were driving to Indiana so he entered the details into their GPS.

He followed the instructions until they came to a bridge.

There were warning signs and road cones but, since the GPS indicated straight ahead, Hussain just drove round them.

He double-checked the GPS, it definitely indicated he should proceed straight ahead.

So he switched off his common sense and relied on technology.

In the dark, he drove straight ahead off the bridge (which ended in mid-air) the car fell forty feet and exploded in a ball of flame.

Hussain survived but his wife did not.

In 2015, in Rio de Janeiro, Francisco Murmura loaded up his car.

He and his wife were headed for the beach, they entered the details into their GPS.

They followed the route but began to have doubts, they were going through a favela.

It felt unsafe, but the GPS was the latest technology, it must know best.

So they switched off their common sense and relied on technology.

They followed the instructions until they were caught up in a gunfight.

Francisco made it out alive, but his wife was shot dead in the crossfire between rival gangs of drug traffickers.

In 2009, in Yorkshire, Robert Jones loaded up his BMW.

He fed the details of his destination into his GPS and followed the instructions.

The GPS took him via a strange route, the roads got very narrow, but the GPS was the latest technology, it must know best.

So he switched off his common sense and relied on technology.

The road became a lane, the lane became a footpath, then the footpath disappeared.

The GPS was still indicating straight ahead when his front wheels went over a cliff.

Police arrived due to reports of a car hanging in mid-air 100 feet above the ground.

Jones was arrested, found guilty of driving without due care and attention, and fined £900.

In 2013, in Belgium, Sabine Moreau loaded up her car.

She was driving 60 kilometres to Brussels and she entered the details into her GPS.

She didn't bother with road signs, she just followed the GPS's instructions.

She didn't need to do anything but drive, the GPS would tell her the best route.

She switched off her common sense and relied on technology.

It took a very long time to cover the 60 kilometres, she had to refuel the car twice, she even had to sleep in it overnight, but eventually she arrived in Brussels.

The route the GPS had taken her had been via Zagreb, Croatia: 1,450 kilometres.

All these people, and thousands more, found technology can't do the thinking for them.

I've done it myself, the GPS has taken me down dead-end streets, or round and round again into endless motorway roadworks.

Eventually, I've had to pull over, turn off the GPS and get out a paper map.

I've had to switch off the technology and switch on my common sense.

But we don't seem to be able to do that in advertising.

Common sense tells us that there's too much bad advertising and people hate it.

But technology tells us our targeting is more efficient than ever and that's all that matters.

I just counted, during an hour-long programme on Sky – 46 ads and promos.

That's 23 minutes an hour, we pay £30 a month and they sell 35% of our time again.

We know current advertising is just pollution, but technology doesn't care about that.

Technology tells us about algorithms and micro-targeting because technology just delivers data, technology doesn't have any common sense.

So if we blindly rely on technology we don't have any common sense either.

WHEN PREPARATION MEETS OPPORTUNITY

In the US, it's manly to take pride in barbecues and grills, and cooking steaks and burgers, and discussing the whole process.

In the summer, the beer ads feature men with ice cold cans of beer, talking about grills as if they were talking about car engines.

This was the market Michael Boehm was interested in when he invented a new grill.

He thought it would be healthier if he slanted the part where the meat was cooked.

That way the melted fat would run off and be collected in a tray beneath.

He tried to sell the idea to Salton, who were a large manufacturer of kitchen products.

They were lukewarm, why hadn't slanted grills been tried before?

If it was a good idea, how come no one had ever done it?

To sell it, they felt they needed a reason why it was different to other grills.

So they launched it as the grill for Mexican food, they named it The Fajita Express.

They showed it at trade shows, but it got a poor reception.

No one saw why they needed a slanted grill for Mexican food, it didn't sell well.

But Boehm knew it was a good product, it just needed decent marketing.

He knew it was healthier, he just needed a way to sell health to men who grilled.

He approached a sports agent and asked if he had a celebrity client who'd be interested in fronting the ads.

And this is the incident the whole story hinges on.

Until now, everything had been logical, and if it had carried on being logical it would have carried on failing.

The agent called up his most glamorous client, the superstar wrestler Hulk Hogan.

Women loved Hogan, so the agent told him he could make a lot of money by lending his name to kitchen products.

Hogan asked what he had in mind, the agent said he had two items: a meatball maker, and a healthy grill.

Hogan thought about it and said: **"Yeah, I like the idea of the first one, we can call it Hulkmania Meatball Maker, let's do it."**

The agent said, okay but what about the grill?

Hogan said, "Nah, my fans aren't interested in barbecues."

So the agent phoned up another of his clients, not as famous as Hulk Hogan, an older one called George Foreman.

George Foreman was the man who'd been beaten by Mohammed Ali in 'The Rumble in the Jungle' many years earlier.

But, after 20 years, he'd made a comeback and regained his World Heavyweight title.

At 45, he was the oldest heavyweight champion in history.

In his career he'd had 73 fights, and he'd won 68 by knockouts.

This was a man other men respected, not some flashy wrestling showboat in glittery trunks.

Because of that phone call, George Foreman began advertising the grill.

They renamed it **'The George Foreman Lean Mean Fat-Reducing Grilling Machine'**.

Now being healthy was okay for guys, not just skinny young men in leotards.

This was health in a way ordinary men, who drank beer while barbecuing steaks, could appreciate.

George Foreman was a smiley, funny, self-deprecating presenter.

And the combination was so incongruous it stood out from everything else around it.

George Foreman sold 100 million grills.

He earned around $200 million, double what he earned in his entire boxing career.

And it was all down to luck.

But, as Michael Boehm knew: **"Luck is when preparation meets opportunity."**

NEVER STOP QUESTIONING

In 1977, Citicorp built their New York headquarters on 53rd and Lexington.

It was 59 stories tall, standing on four nine-story-high stilts, with a 45-degree angled roof.

It was on stilts because they couldn't move the Church at ground level.

They couldn't build on the plot, so they had to build in the airspace above.

And, because of the Church, the stilts couldn't be placed at the corners, where they'd be strongest, they had to be placed at the sides.

So the angled roof was a 400-ton tuned mass-damper to compensate for movement.

A Princeton structural engineering student, Diane Hartley, decided to write her thesis on it.

She went to the company that built it, William LeMessurier was the structural engineer.

A junior engineer, Joel Weinstein, gave her access to all calculations and blueprints.

They even offered her a $10,000 stipend to let them use her thesis for a book.

She was thrilled, until she began going through the numbers.

She just couldn't make them add up the way the structural engineers had.

According to her, they only calculated for high winds to strike at the sides, which was fine if the stilts were at the corners.

But they weren't, the stilts were at the side, and when she calculated the effect of the wind on the corners the strength was 60% of what their calculations said.

She called the junior engineer back and asked how this was possible.

He mumbled something about the columns being strong enough, then hung up.

She checked the numbers then she called back, but no one would take her call.

Even when she called to discuss the stipend for the book, they wouldn't call her back.

She kept trying, but eventually she just gave up and got on with her life.

She never knew what happened after her call, and why no one ever called her back.

She wouldn't find out for 20 years.

In fact, her query worked its way up to the top of the engineering firm, where they found her calculations were right and theirs were wrong.

They panicked and realised they had erected a building that could fail in high winds.

If the building fell it could kill thousands of people.

The panic was the realisation that the 200 main bolts in the building could fail.

The bolts had to have two-inch-thick steel plates welded over them, it took two months.

To avoid a panic the work was done in secret, at night, without anyone knowing.

The NYPD stood ready to evacuate a 10-block radius, 2,000 Red Cross personnel were on standby, and three weather services were monitored 24/7.

Luckily, the newspapers were on strike, and a predicted hurricane never arrived.

And everyone was sworn to secrecy, so nobody said a word.

Until 20 years later, in 1995 Joe Morgenstern overheard the story at a party.

He investigated it and wrote it up for *New Yorker* magazine.

PBS read his exposé and turned it into an astonishing documentary.

And one night, nearly 20 years after she graduated, Diane Hartley's husband called her downstairs to watch TV saying: **"Honey, you won't believe this."**

Which is when she found the reason why the structural engineers never returned her calls.

What she had spotted was something that the people who built the building didn't spot.

And they were so involved in keeping it a secret, they wouldn't talk to anyone.

But now, at least she knows that questioning those numbers saved thousands of lives.

And that's why we should learn the value of speaking up and asking questions.

We shouldn't assume senior people know more than we do.

However big, and powerful, and experienced, and infallible we think they are.

However frightened we are of looking silly.

If we don't understand something the worst thing we can do is to stay silent.

As Diane Hartley says: **"We should never stop questioning."**

WE CAN'T OWN KNOWLEDGE

A few years back, famous chef Nigella Lawson suggested using cream in spaghetti carbonara.

Immediately **'foodies'** were outraged.

Didn't she know that you must never, EVER use cream in carbonara, the egg yolks are what gives it its creamy taste?

She's supposed to be a chef, what is she thinking of?

Everyone immediately jumped all over her for desecrating an age-old Italian recipe.

One headline read: **"An outrage to Italian cuisine: Nigella Lawson angers Italians with her controversial carbonara recipe."**

Social media was more pointed: **"Nigella you are a wonderful woman but your recipes are the DEATH of Italian recipes, literally! NO CREAM IN CARBONARA NEVER, only eggs."**

And again: **"Nigella, there are many cuisines in the world that need tarting up with cream, the best cuisine in the world, namely Italian does not need you to ruin it."**

And again: **"Cubed pancetta? White wine? Double cream? Parmesan cheese? This is not carbonara, this is a real MERDA! Te pudeat!"**

All the self-proclaimed experts weighed in to protect the authentic, age-old Italian recipe.

There is just one problem.

Spaghetti carbonara isn't an authentic, age-old Italian recipe.

It was invented in 1944 for the American troops that were liberating Rome.

The soldiers were getting bored with the same old K-rations every day.

They wanted something new and interesting, but minestrone soup just wasn't enough.

The soldiers had lots of eggs and bacon, the Italians had lots of pasta.

Between them, they found a way to put these together, and carbonara was born.

Everyone, Americans and Italians, loved it, but even at the beginning there were differences of opinion on the recipe.

Some preferred rigatoni, some preferred spaghetti.

Some preferred pancetta (pork belly) some preferred guanciale (pork jowl).

Some preferred pecorino, some preferred parmesan.

Some preferred it with onions, some without.

So everyone originally had their own style, but a few years later 'foodies' are acting as if there has only ever been one authentic style throughout all of history.

Not only are they wrong, they're missing the point.

The point is to make delicious food, not to recreate a piece of history.

But these are people who believe their *subjective* opinion is the only *objective* reality.

We have many people like this in our business.

I recently wrote on Twitter that I liked the thinking behind the Fever Tree campaign:

'75% OF YOUR GIN & TONIC IS MIXER, SHOULDN'T YOU BUY THE BEST MIXER?'

I thought it was an interesting approach: **"You're paying a lot for the best gin, why spoil the G&T by saving money on the cheapest part?"**

It reminded me of Theodore Levitt's quote: **"Last year, a million quarter inch drills were sold. Not because people wanted quarter inch drills but because people wanted quarter inch holes."**

I thought it was an interesting way for Fever Tree to take market share for their brand.

But I immediately got several comments like this:

"75% is far too much tonic, what a waste."

"You should never mix G&T more than 60/40."

"I never mix tonic more than 50/50 with gin, it ruins the gin."

All comments about gin drinking, not marketing – subjective not objective.

(And these are supposed to be marketing professionals.)

Years ago at BMP, we used to refer to remarks like that as going, **"Straight to the heart of the trivia."**

Which seems to me to be where much of advertising is headed.

MONEY: BY-PRODUCT OR END-PRODUCT?

Recently, it started raining money in California.

On a northbound interstate highway, an armoured car was transporting sacks full of $1 and $20 bills when the back doors came open.

The sacks fell out and burst, and the turbulence created by the fast traffic caused the money to fly in the air like confetti.

That's unusual, fair enough, but what happened next was jaw-dropping.

Drivers hit their brakes without thinking, they made emergency stops in the middle of the highway, where traffic was doing 70 mph.

They flung open the doors and abandoned their cars and started scrabbling on the tarmac to grab notes, clutching them out of the air, off the road, whooping and screaming.

The second they saw the money they just lost all rational thought, stopped their cars where they were and started snatching at it.

More and more drivers joined in, more and more cars were backed up along the highway.

Luckily no one was hurt, but the drivers on the ground were oblivious anyway, the instant they saw the money all rational thought left their heads.

I like money as much as anyone, but FFS use your brain.

Supposing you manage to grab twenty $20 bills, that's $400.

Meanwhile, the car that you've abandoned in the middle of the highway gets totalled by a massive truck, that'll cost you around $20,000.

Or supposing your car causes a wreck in which someone dies, or supposing while you're on your knees grabbing money you get hit by a truck and die.

You can't grab enough $20 bills to pay for that.

But for some people the sight of free money supersedes everything else.

See, here's the thing about money, it isn't magic – those bits of paper have no actual value themselves, the only value they have is what you can exchange them for.

So before you stop the car and scrabble around on the road just think for a millisecond, are those few bills worth what it could cost?

I could maybe understand if this was a rundown section of town where people had nothing, but it wasn't, it was an interstate highway full of expensive cars.

And people with a belief that money was magic tokens that automatically delivered everything you could possibly desire.

Some of those people just slammed their car door with the keys inside as they ran to grab the money, so the cars were locked on the highway and couldn't be moved.

The police arrested them and had the cars towed away, the fines amounting to more than whatever they collected.

The police used the news media to explain that this wasn't free money, it was theft.

"If a truck carrying TV sets drops them on the highway, you can't just grab the TVs and take them away", a spokesman said.

But money is like a drug that bypasses the brain.

The police explained there was lots of footage of car number plates and the faces of the people taking the money, if the money wasn't returned in 48 hours those people faced prosecution.

Gradually, reluctantly, some of the money began to trickle back.

People tend to see money as an end-point, the standard that all things must be measured against, the final goal.

But for us, it doesn't make sense to just chase money.

If we do great work money will follow, so it makes sense to chase the work.

But I've seen people chase the money – they were doing great work, so they got offered more money elsewhere, so they left and went for the money.

Suddenly they weren't doing such great work anymore, so the money dried up, now they don't have the work or the money.

See, if you've got great work you've got a great portfolio, and that will always sell.

But if all you have is the fact that you used to earn a lot of money, well you can't put that in your portfolio.

Hence, money is a by-product not an end-product – QED.

TALKING INTO A MIRROR

In 1985, Sting released the track **'Russians'**.

It was the height of the Cold War and the song summed up nuclear hysteria.

It began with an ominous intro by Prokofiev, and then the main chorus was: **"I hope the Russians love their children, too."**

One of the lines was, **"Mr Khrushchev said: 'We will bury you.'"**

This was a famous quote that had fuelled the dread of nuclear war for thirty years.

The only problem was, it was a misquote, inasmuch as it wasn't what Khrushchev meant.

In 1956, Khrushchev was addressing western diplomats and he used the phrase: **"My vas pokhronim."**

This was translated by his personal translator, Viktor Sukhodrev, as: **"We will bury you."**

This phrase was extracted from that speech and headlined across western media for the next three decades, it showed Russia just wanted to rain nuclear missiles down on us.

This is a perfect example of trying to communicate while living in separate bubbles.

Khrushchev lived in the bubble of communism, for him the struggle wasn't between countries, the struggle was between ideologies, between the workers and the ruling classes.

That was the world Khrushchev lived in, he naturally assumed the entire world was as familiar with the works of Karl Marx as everyone in the USSR was.

That everyone knew the famous quote from *The Communist Manifesto*: **"The proletariat is the undertaker (gravedigger) of capitalism."**

Khrushchev wasn't referring to the East versus the West, he was referring to the working class versus the ruling class.

He was referencing the phrase: **"Workers of all countries unite, oppose our common enemy."**

But of course that wasn't how it was heard by people in the West, who never read *The Communist Manifesto*, and it wasn't how it was used by newspapers in need of a headline.

Khrushchev himself recognised the misunderstanding when it was too late.

In 1963, in Yugoslavia, he said: **"I once said, 'We will bury you,' and I got into trouble with it. Of course we will not bury you with a shovel. Your own working class will bury you."**

Khrushchev's complete sentence was: **"Whether you like it or not, we are on the right side of history. We will bury you."**

In 2018, *New York Times* translator, Mark Polizzotti, said that while the words may have been translated exactly, the sense was misleading.

What would have been more accurate was the phrase: **"We will outlast you."**

That's something we should learn, a translator's job is not just to literally take one set of words and simply pass them on.

A translator's job should be to understand the two different sets of circumstances, different sets of experiences, of expectations, of meanings.

To *translate* one meaning into the other.

Viktor Sukhodrev was recognised as one of the best interpreters; as he was dying he summed up his career: **"They formulated it. I just interpreted it."**

But everyone recognises that in that case, he got it wrong.

He literally translated the exact words, but he didn't *interpret* the meaning.

His mistake poured fuel on a situation that could have led to war.

What we do, thankfully, couldn't lead to anything like that.

But we should learn from Viktor Sukhodrev.

Learn that we are useless unless we can empathise with the state of mind of the person receiving our communication.

It's not just our job to *speak* correctly, it's our job to make sure we're *heard* correctly.

GAMING THE DATA

In 1937, Robert McNamara graduated from university with a BA in economics, maths, and philosophy: a dangerous combination.

He then got an MBA from Harvard and taught accounting; he became their highest-paid and youngest assistant professor.

In 1943, he joined the Army, teaching analytical business approaches, to soldiers.

Then he became a colonel in the Air Force at the Office of Statistical Control.

In 1946, he joined Ford, running planning, and management control systems.

He led Ford in adopting computers; what he called **'Scientific Management'.**

He was so good at it he became President of Ford.

He was a brilliant man who knew the answer to everything lay solely in data analysis.

In 1960 he was recruited by President Kennedy to be Secretary of Defence.

Via computer modelling, he did the job by spreadsheets, graphs, and trends.

His data convinced him that the war in Vietnam was going well.

In 1962, he said: **"Every quantitative measurement shows me we are winning the war."**

According to McNamara's projections the war would be over by 1964.

But by 1965, the war wasn't over, in fact America was losing.

McNamara's data analysis consistently showed the only way to win was for America to escalate the war.

So much so, that in government it became known as **'McNamara's War'.**

He knew the metrics wouldn't lie, so he decided the way to prove they were winning was by a superior body count: kill more of the enemy.

So 'body count' became the most important metric on the spreadsheet, that would prove that the US was winning, numbers don't lie.

And so the main goal of every military unit was to achieve the highest body count.

But McNamara's quantitative style, based on number-crunching by computers, missed the human dimension.

General William Peers wrote: **"With improper leadership, 'body count' could create competition between units, particularly if these statistics were compared like baseball standings and there were no stringent requirements as to how and by whom the counts were to be made."**

The obsession with body counts meant promotions for officers with larger numbers, which led to exaggeration of enemy losses.

Soldiers would claim kills that hadn't been made, officers would inflate those numbers, and so on up the chain of command.

If the top brass just wanted numbers, they'd get numbers.

So the data was useless because it was based on lies.

But whatever the evidence of common sense, McNamara wouldn't be swayed from his belief in statistics and data.

Senator Richard Russell said: **"McNamara is the smartest fellow any of us know, but he's opinionated as hell and he's made up his mind."**

Eventually, even McNamara admitted the models and stats he attached such importance to were **"grossly in error"** and he was **"now pretty well convinced that our present policy can lead only to disastrous defeat."**

But that's what happens when we have the arrogance to depend purely on data and computers to tell us how the world will behave.

Because people will always game the system, any system.

So when we create a system, we are creating something to be gamed.

And if it can be gamed, it will be gamed.

We need to learn, we mustn't confuse algorithms with brains.

PART 9

SELLING IDEAS v IDEAS THAT SELL

ZOHNERISM

In 1997, Nathan Zohner wrote a paper as part of his school science project.

It was called **"How Gullible Are We?"**

He circulated it amongst his classmates.

It started with information about Dihydrogen Monoxide (DHMO for short), which was a compound found in every river, stream, lake, and reservoir in America.

Its accidental ingestion had been implicated in the deaths of thousands of Americans every year.

In gaseous form DHMO could cause severe burns.

Further dangers were as follows:

DHMO is the main component of acid rain, contributing to erosion of the natural landscape.

It accelerates corrosion and rusting in many metals.

It may cause electrical failures, and decreased effectiveness in automobile brakes.

For everyone with a dependency on DHMO, total withdrawal can lead to death.

Then Nathan Zohner listed the places DHMO was found:

As an industrial solvent and coolant, in nuclear power plants.

In the production of Styrofoam, and as a fire retardant.

In the distribution of pesticides, and as an additive in certain 'junk foods'.

At the end, he added a questionnaire, he asked his classmates to vote on what action they thought should be taken as regards DHMO.

43 of his 50 classmates (86%) voted to ban DHMO immediately.

His classmates were science students, their parents worked in the local science-related industries.

They were invited to research DHMO for themselves, even ask their teachers about it.

But none did.

Which is a shame, because they could have checked the etymology of its full name: dihydrogen monoxide.

'Di' means two – so that's two atoms of hydrogen, 'mono' means one – so that's one atom of oxygen: two atoms of hydrogen to one atom of oxygen.

Another way of writing that would be H_2O, still another way would be **'water'**.

His classmates had voted to ban water.

What made Nathan Zohner's paper really interesting was that this group were far more educated about science than the average person.

All they were presented with were the simple facts, and yet they were persuaded to ban the one substance that was absolutely vital for life on the planet.

Remember the title of his paper was **"How Gullible Are We?"**

But before we turn our noses up and call his paper a deception, remember it's the same language we use every day.

"You can't buy a better butter", maybe, but this is what's called a 'top parity claim'.

We imply we're the best, but actually we just say we're as good as anyone else.

"Can help with weight loss as part of your calorie-controlled diet", well duh, if you're on a calorie-controlled diet anything that's part of it will help with weight loss.

"Too much sugar can be harmful", well yes it can, but so can too many carrots.

The right amount of sugar can be as healthy as the right amount of anything.

"Our finest bread ever", it may well be the finest bread WE'VE made, but that doesn't mean it's better than anyone else's.

"Made by the nicest people in the world", of course we have no way of knowing if this is true, but it falls into the category of 'advertising puffery'.

Advertising puffery is defined as: **"Broad, exaggerated or boastful statements that are a matter of opinion rather than a fact, and which no reasonable person would assume to be literally true."**

Without lying, we allow people to infer what we want them to believe.

ALL MAYONNAISE AND NO SALAD

When Charlie Sheen was young, he lived for pleasure, mainly drugs and sex.

He had a budding film career, but work took second place to an orgy of hedonism, literally.

Naturally, this ended up in the courts, which means it ended up in the news media, which means his film career pretty much ended up.

Charlie Sheen's drug-taking and use of prostitutes was beyond scandalous.

In court, a judge commented, **"So you pay these women fifty thousand dollars a month for sex?"**

Charlie Sheen simply answered, **"No, I pay them fifty thousand dollars to leave after sex."**

Even his father commented on his lifestyle.

He said Charlie hadn't understood that life was like a salad: you have lettuce, tomatoes, and cucumber, that's the salad but on its own it's pretty tasteless.

So you add mayonnaise, which gives the salad taste.

He said Charlie had confused the salad with the mayonnaise.

He knew the mayonnaise tasted great so he didn't bother with the salad, he just wanted a plate of mayonnaise.

So that was the way he lived his life, all mayonnaise and no salad.

But that wasn't the way to make a salad, and that's what Charlie would have to learn.

Which is pretty much where we in advertising find ourselves, all mayonnaise and no salad.

Many years back, when advertising started it was just information repeated over and over.

Boring and tasteless: like a salad without dressing.

So, to make it palatable, we added some dressing.

We added good music, good lighting, good editing, good casting.

Then we added emotion, and purpose, and warmth, and social responsibility.

Then we added planning, and strategy, and data, and algorithms.

And we never noticed that there wasn't anything about the product anymore, we had a large plate of mayonnaise and no salad.

All mood and no content, all emotion and no reason, all heart and no brain, all brand and no product, all taste and no substance.

And we can't seem to understand why it isn't working.

We make lots of nice little films with good music, good filming, good voices.

The voices make points about peace, and love, and responsibility, and hope.

They don't mention anything as crass as the thing being sold, what it is, what it does, why you should buy it, why it's better than anything else.

We got rid of the boring part, the salad, and kept the tasty part, the mayonnaise, it should be even better.

We can't seem to understand that advertising, like a salad, needs both.

Advertising is delivery system.

The point is to deliver information, to do it in an interesting, enjoyable way because that makes people more likely to notice and remember what we're delivering.

But if we forget *what* we're delivering, if we only concentrate on the enjoyable part, we lose the whole point of doing it.

Like putting beautiful wrapping paper on an empty box: it looks great but when you open it up there's nothing inside.

It's not our job to deliver empty boxes, even if the wrapping paper wins awards.

We know a box that's attractively wrapped is more likely to get opened, that's the only reason for making the boxes attractive.

We come, uninvited, into people's lives; nobody wants advertising, that's why we have to make the experience enjoyable, of course.

But there needs to be some salad with the mayonnaise.

ADVERTISING ISN'T SELLING

Most of us know about the trademark row between Duracell and Energizer.

But the most important part is the part most of us don't know.

Brief recap: in 1972, Duracell launched its alkaline battery.

They demonstrated it in an ad featuring a lot of toy drumming bunnies.

Gradually all the bunnies stopped drumming, except Duracell.

The ad was successful and Duracell became market leader.

But in the early 1980s they forgot to renew the copyright on the drumming bunny.

Energizer quickly copyrighted the drumming bunny and ran their own parody commercial.

It said Duracell's commercial hadn't featured Energizer because it lasted longer.

This time all the bunnies stopped except the Energizer one.

And Duracell couldn't use the bunny to answer because Energizer owned the copyright.

That's the story most of us know, but we don't know the part that happened next.

It demonstrates the world of advertising hubris most of us live in.

When Energizer ran that ad, their sales went down and Duracell sales went up.

That's right, the Energizer commercial with the drumming bunny actually put UP sales for its competitor, Duracell.

How could that be?

Well, although everyone in advertising watches every ad in microscopic detail and is keenly aware of who is running what, the general public couldn't care less.

All they remember is that Duracell had a drumming bunny, so the ad must be for them.

Consequently, when they get to the store that's what they buy.

Energizer quickly identified the problem, the ad was generating lots of awareness but it wasn't carrying it through to purchase.

Whoever owns top-of-mind gets the sale.

So Energizer put the drumming bunny on their packs and on all their point-of-sale.

Now consumers didn't have to remember who owned the bunny, there it was on the pack, right at point-of-purchase.

Energizer sales immediately took off, and that's what I mean about advertising hubris.

The part that everyone who lives for advertising awards sees as demeaning, point-of-sale, is actually what moves product.

Because that's where the consumer actually picks it up, that's where money actually changes hands.

TV advertising only does awareness, which is why brand purpose manifestos masquerading as TV commercials are dumb.

Expecting people to concentrate on the TV ad so hard that they don't even need to remember the name of the brand, just the emotion the ad generated.

This is breath-taking arrogance, not joined-up thinking.

'Joined-up thinking' was originally called TTL: through-the-line (to be a campaign it had to work below-the-line as well as above-the-line).

A great example of this is for Fram oil filters in the US.

It doesn't matter if you don't remember the name of the brand, because they have the spokesperson, the actor who plays Mike Ehrmantraut from *Breaking Bad*, saying over the packshot: **"It's the orange one, numb nuts."**

That's a great example of TTL advertising at work.

You don't have to remember the name, but you'll remember that line.

And when you're in the store, about to pick up an oil filter, all you have to do is to pick out the orange one.

Why would you remember that line?

Well the audience is young men who work on cars and that's their language, numb nuts.

ARE WE SELLING THE FOREST OR THE TREES?

In America in 1991, Subaru were small and they weren't growing.

The problem was, compared to Toyota and Nissan, they had no image.

Subaru felt, in order to compete, they would need a similar mainstream image.

This is standard, dumb advertising thinking.

It never occurred to Subaru that Toyota and Nissan were many times bigger, and that copying them would just be seen as a poor imitation.

You can't beat someone by copying them.

But Subaru wanted to look like the big boys, so they wanted advertising that made them feel like a big mainstream brand.

So that was Subaru's brief to the ad agencies pitching for their account.

Each agency pitched with a strapline that would be the backbone for its campaign.

Wieden & Kennedy pitched with: SUBARU: WHAT TO DRIVE.

DCA pitched with: SUBARU. THE PERFECT CAR FOR AN IMPERFECT WORLD.

Warwick, Baker and Fiore pitched with: SUBARU. CARS THAT CAN.

Jordan McGrath pitched with: SUBARU. FOR ALL THE RIGHT REASONS.

W.B. Doner pitched with: GET REAL, GET A SUBARU.

W.B. Doner also pitched a second campaign: THE SUBARU STORY, IT NEVER ENDS.

Levine, Huntley, Schmidt & Beaver pitched: THE CAR THAT WILL CHANGE YOUR MIND.

All of those campaign lines were the product of consumer research.

They were all meant to reflect the type of driver who was right for Subaru.

Sensible, no-nonsense, practical, unpretentious.

So they made the car fit the audience, not the other way round.

They decided the audience were the brand, so they sold the audience back to itself.

There is one major flaw in that approach.

It gives the client a nice warm feeling because it feels like Toyota or Nissan advertising, but that's exactly the problem with it.

That advertising could be for anyone, take out the Subaru name and you could substitute Toyota or Nissan.

And both of those brands have many times Subaru's share-of-mind, so that advertising won't change a thing in the market.

The agency that won the account was Wieden & Kennedy.

The advertising obviously failed, W&K were fired and so were the Subaru marketing department.

The new management woke up to reality, Subaru were not a mass-market brand the size of Toyota or Nissan, they were a challenger brand and had better start acting like it.

Nothing was going to change by talking about consumer image, brand advertising.

Product builds image, image builds brand.

They needed to talk about what made their CAR different from other CARS.

They hired a Texas agency, Temerlin McClain, who built a campaign around what made Subaru cars different: SUBARU. THE BEAUTY OF ALL-WHEEL DRIVE.

The ads demonstrated that Subaru is the only car, apart from Porsche, with a flat-six engine, a straight-line symmetric drivetrain, and all-wheel drive.

They reframed AWD as *the ultimate safety feature* because of its incredible road-holding.

Inside a year, the Subaru station wagon was the best-selling station wagon in America.

Within a decade, Subaru sales had increased 700%.

As George Muller, the new president, said: **"It goes all the way back to the engineers who designed our product and why they designed it the way they did."**

Imagine, selling an actual product would work better than selling brand purpose?

As George Orwell said, **"To see what's in front of one's nose requires constant struggle."**

WHO'S THE GREATER FOOL?

In 2003, two Spanish brothers bought a painting, a Goya, worth 250,000 Euros.

It was a bargain, so they made a 20,000 Euro down payment and collected the picture.

They knew it was genuine because it had a certificate of authenticity.

It didn't occur to them that if someone could fake a painting they could also fake a certificate of authenticity.

Which is exactly what happened, and an expert declared that the painting and the certificate of authenticity were both fakes.

But the brothers knew they were smarter than most people.

If the forgeries were good enough to fool them, then they were certainly good enough to fool anyone else.

The brothers met a man who worked for an Arab Sheikh, he said the Sheikh would be interested in buying their Goya, the brothers said the price was 4 million Euros.

The man said he would want a fee of 300,000 Euros for arranging the sale.

They met in Turin, the man brought a suitcase with 1.7 million Euros as down payment on the painting.

The brothers drove home via Switzerland but, when they got to the French border, customs officials opened the suitcase and found the money was all fake.

The brothers had been paid 1.7 million Euros in forged notes.

Without telling the brothers, the French authorities phoned the Spanish authorities, and when the brothers returned to Spain they were arrested for smuggling counterfeit currency.

The only genuine money was the 300,000 Euros they'd paid the middle man, which they had borrowed and were now in debt for.

The brothers had been stupid to buy a fake painting in the first place.

But their bigger mistake was thinking that other people would be as stupid as them.

They thought they were smarter than everyone else so they could fool other people.

In financial markets this is known as the **'Greater Fool'** theory.

Someone buys a stock, finds it is worthless, then believes they can find someone more stupid than them to sell it to, a **'greater fool'** in fact.

A bubble happens when everyone believes this will continue, and the market carries on growing until it runs out of fools, at which point it collapses.

This is what is happening in advertising.

We know what we are doing is fake, but we don't think anyone else will know.

Current marketing thinking is **'brand purpose'** advertising.

This is just a complicated way of saying, whatever we're selling, let's pretend it will change people's lives, they're dumb enough to believe it.

But why should people believe it, when we don't believe it ourselves?

There isn't a single person sitting in an advertising agency anywhere that truly believes a product will help you FIND YOUR NOW or LIVE YOUR DREAM or BE YOUR TRUTH.

They don't believe it, but they expect ordinary people to swallow it.

Before he was a comedian, Jimmy Carr used to work in advertising.

When he graduated from Cambridge he became an account man, and he puts it like this:

"Adverts used to be about products. They would tell you what the product did and you would either need that thing or you wouldn't need that thing. Real simple.

But then there was a shift in emphasis, a sleight of hand.

Now the advert is selling you a desire – power, success, peace of mind.

They pick a desire and they say 'If you had this, then you'd have that.'"

We know we're selling things we don't actually believe ourselves, but we think consumers will believe it.

And yet we know that, *before* we got into advertising, we were just consumers ourselves, and we didn't believe it then.

So who's really the greater fool?

DEPRIVATION MARKETING

Jeff Goodby and Rich Silverstein were pitching for the California Milk Processing Board.

For years, the advertising had been: **"Milk, it does a body good"**.

But this was old news, everyone knew milk made strong teeth and bones.

As Carl Ally said: **"Advertising should make the new familiar and the familiar new."**

In this case they needed to do the latter, make people reappraise milk.

Jon Steel was the planner and he ran some focus groups before the briefing.

For a week before the groups, he asked the participants to stop using milk.

Then he asked them what it had been like.

One man's experience was typical: **"I came down in the morning, poured out my cereal and sliced a banana on it like usual then I remembered, no milk. Now what could I do, pour the cereal back in the box, I can't use soda or Gatorade or water?"**

Eventually one woman summed it up: **"You don't really notice milk until it's gone."**

Jon Steel wrote that down as the brief.

To demonstrate the strategy at the pitch, they put a video camera inside the agency fridge and filmed staff when they discovered there was no milk.

They'd have to have their coffee or sandwich or cake without, their faces dropped

A planner asked Jeff Goodby what title he wanted on the deck, he said: **"I dunno, maybe just 'Got milk?'"**

The planner said: **"Surely 'Got ENOUGH milk?' makes more sense?"**

Goodby said: **"Nah, I prefer it shorter, it's catchier."**

During the pitch, Goodby was thinking maybe **'Got milk?'** might make a good strapline.

After the pitch they gave the client a booklet with their thinking, and photos of the agency team and, just for a laugh, each of them had a little milk moustache.

The planner, Jon Steel, said: **"You know that would make a great campaign, celebrities with milk moustaches."**

Jeff Goodby said: **"Nah, it doesn't fit with the idea of food needing milk."**

So the agency ran the campaign they'd pitched: people unable to eat peanut butter, or cookies, or chocolate cake without milk, and they used the strapline: **'Got milk?'**

It was a massive success.

Then the Milk Processing Education Program decided to do national advertising.

An agency called Bozell launched a campaign with celebrities with milk moustaches, but they used the strapline: **'Milk, what a surprise.'**

The visuals were a huge hit, but the strapline was dull and forgettable.

The client made them change it to the hugely successful: **'Got milk?'**

Suddenly celebrities wanted to be photographed wearing a milk moustache, and Annie Leibovitz wanted to photograph them: Harrison Ford, Elton John, Muhammed Ali, Jackie Chan, Spike Lee, Danny DeVito, Whoopi Goldberg, The Simpsons, Kermit the Frog: 350 ads and 70 commercials over 20 years.

People even adapted the line for their own uses: Got Cakes? Got Jesus? Got Bacon? Got Burritos? Got Raisins? Got Muscles? Got Balls? Got Teeth? Got Gas? Got Porn?

Oreo even imprinted **'Got Milk?'** straight onto their cookies.

All because ordinary people spotted what a planner, Jon Steel, had spotted before a single ad had run.

When something is part of life, the way to get people to notice it is to take it away.

And the way to make that noticeable is to have fun and not take yourself seriously.

Jon Steel went on to write the best-selling book: *Truth, Lies, and Advertising*.

My favourite quote of his is: **"The best attribute a planner can have is to be useful."**

The same way there aren't many great creatives, there aren't many great planners.

TOOLBOX IN A SPRAY CAN

My art director partner, Gordon Smith, once told me he was driving through flood water in the country when he saw someone he knew, stuck.

It was Andrew Cracknel, ECD of WCRS, who was also in a Range Rover.

Andrew said his engine was wet and wouldn't start.

So Gordon took Andrew's sparkplugs out and sprayed WD40 on them, then he put them back and Andrew's engine started.

I said that was amazing, I didn't know WD40 could do that.

Gordon said the name WD40 stood for Water Displacement formula 40.

So it dispersed water which was why it got the wet sparkplug to work.

WD40 was developed in 1953 to protect the Atlas missile from rust and corrosion.

I was online recently when an ad came up: "Get gum out of your hair with WD40".

I thought, that's amazing, I thought the only way to get gum out of hair was with scissors.

A bit later I saw another ad: "Stop your windscreen icing up with WD40".

I thought that's a great idea, it would save me scraping the ice off every morning.

Then later still, I saw another ad: "Get paint and scratches off your car with WD40".

I'd previously bought a bottle of Liquid Scratch Repair Kit on the internet, it didn't work.

So I sprayed some WD40 on the scratches on my car and rubbed, and it came up perfectly.

Next time I saw a WD40 ad in my feed I clicked it and went to a site with **58** different uses for WD40.

Everything from cleaning stains off the toilet bowl, to fixing cracked screens on iPhones, to getting burns and stains out of carpets, to destroying wasps nests, to dissolving superglue, to cleaning BBQ grills, to removing coffee or wine stains, to getting crayon marks off the wall, to removing oil stains from the driveway, to protecting leather sofas, to getting rings unstuck from fingers, to making your fridge gasket last longer, to cleaning your hands.

There are several brilliant pieces of thinking here.

First, everyone has at least one can of WD40 in their house, shed, or garage.

They bought it once and only use it when something is rusty or stuck.

They'll never replace it unless it runs out, and it won't run out unless they use it.

So this is a great way to get people to think of new uses for their existing can of WD40 and need to replace it.

Which makes it a great campaign for *high-involvement* consumers.

Second, it speaks to all the people who never bought a can of WD40.

This tells them that it's so much more than just oil.

The 58 different uses show something for everyone, from teenagers to old ladies.

So it's also a great campaign for *low-involvement* consumers.

Finally, the media is a terrific fit.

Instead of a brand ad on TV, online media gives them the flexibility and the ubiquity to target their users and deliver much more information than they could get in 30 seconds of TV, at a fraction of the price.

This is a really smart use of online media, because it uses the media for everything other media can't do.

Instead of just using TV commercials online, as pre-rolls which get skipped after five seconds.

This way, cookies track your audience and you know which messages to serve individuals.

Each of the uses is a 10-second read to an interested audience.

The cumulative effect is like a long infomercial full of useful information.

You're talking to someone who actually wants the information you've got to tell them.

So the emotional build you're left with is a powerful brand campaign.

THAT'S using online for something you couldn't do in any other media.

WHAT WE *WANT* VERSUS WHAT WE *NEED*

My big sister is 11 years older than me, she was a teenager in the 1950s.

Like most teenagers she used to go out with her friends on Saturday nights.

My dad was a police sergeant and quite strict, especially where young girls were concerned.

So he'd want to know where she was going before she went out.

Shirley told him she was going dancing at Ilford Palais, she was wearing a wide pink below-the-knee skirt, lots of petticoats underneath, with a poodle embroidered on it, also a pink angora cardigan, all very ladylike.

Once she left the house she went to Barking tube station and into the Ladies' room.

She changed into tight black peddle-pusher leggings, a black polo-neck top, black pump shoes, and dark glasses.

Then she got the tube into Soho and went to the basement jazz clubs where she danced to Ken Collier, Si Lori, or Chris Barber's jazz bands.

On the way home, she'd stop at Barking tube station and do the same thing in reverse, so when she came home she was wearing all the cute pink clothes Dad saw her go out in.

Dad was happy that Shirley had a nice, safe time dancing at Ilford Palais.

Shirley was happy that she'd had a great time dancing in basement jazz clubs in Soho.

Everyone was happy and there was no need for a row.

Everyone got what they wanted.

This used to be the role of the best account handlers at the best ad agencies.

To make sure everyone got what they want.

Paul Simons once put it to me like this:

"The client knows what they want. The agency knows what they need.

It's the account handler's job to get the client to want what they need."

The client's job is marketing, not advertising.

Advertising is just one of about a dozen things the client has to do.

So they can't possibly do it was well as someone who's concentrating on it 100%.

It's just a part of the client's job, so mainly they want to make sure it doesn't go wrong.

The safest way to do that is to make sure it looks like all the other advertising in their sector.

Don't take risks, but of course with that attitude it becomes part of the wallpaper.

If you're the market leader this is not a problem, if you're not it's a waste of money.

As a client you haven't got time to concentrate on what needs to be done to make all your ads look different, to stand out.

So you need someone who has that as their whole job, in other words you need a good ad agency to do that for you.

But of course, you may not immediately like the result, simply because it looks different from everything in your sector.

As a client, you *want* what makes your life easier, there's a lot of reassurance in that.

But what you *want*, what makes your life easy, isn't in your brand's best interests.

Because what will work will make you feel uncomfortable, so it won't be what you *want*.

That's why the best account handlers' jobs were to get the client to feel comfortable with something that would normally make them uncomfortable.

Knowing that when the results were in, the sales figures were what would actually count.

And that would be the final basis for the client's judgement of the ads.

Not, **"Did I like it?"** but, **"Did it work?"**

As Maggie Thatcher said to Tim Bell: **"I don't like the advertising. But you're supposed to be the experts so I suppose I'd better let you get on with it."**

With that attitude, she and Saatchi & Saatchi won three elections in a row.

AN ADVERTISING STORY

In 1950, radio was the biggest entertainment medium, every family listened to it.

The programme most families listened to was *Dick Barton Special Agent* at 6.45 pm.

It was a typical cliff-hanger, every episode ended with Dick Barton about to die, only for him to have miraculously escaped by the next episode.

At the same time, the BBC was producing radio programmes for farmers.

These programmes were like the print magazines: *Farmer's Weekly* and *Stock Breeder*.

They were full of speciality news about prices, crops, markets, new techniques; they were dry and technical information only farmers would be interested in.

But the BBC was a public broadcaster, so they needed to make programmes for everyone.

Godfrey Basely was given the task of creating a farming programme that would be relevant to farmers but wouldn't be too dull for non-farmers.

He went to the Midlands for a conference among farming folk about the problem.

One farmer, Henry Birt from Lincolnshire, farmed blackcurrants and seed crops and he said one thunderstorm could wipe out his entire crop, he said farming wasn't boring in fact it could be terrifying with all the suspense of a cliff-hanger.

He said, **"You ought to make a farming programme like that Dick Barton show"** and everyone laughed, except Godfrey Basely.

Because that combination became the birth of an entirely new kind of broadcasting.

Basely saw that although he couldn't combine farming with a thriller, he could combine farming information with the lives of ordinary farming folks.

So he began a radio show that was 10% specific advice related to crops plus 30% general agriculture and horticultural content, and 60% stories about the lives of country folk.

He began with three families: one was a poor but modern farmer, one was a poor and old-fashioned farmer, and one was a well-off bigger farmer.

And that was how the first episode of *The Archers* started in January 1951, it began by delivering farming information interwoven with stories.

But would it work, interweaving information with stories?

Well, 70 years later *The Archers* is getting close to its 20,000th episode; at its highest point it had 20 million listeners.

Even today it still has 5 million listeners (a million of those on the internet) and although *The Archers* is only on radio, it has a bigger audience than *Coronation Street*'s 4 million viewers and *EastEnders'* 2.7 million viewers, both on TV.

So it seems the public does enjoy information interweaved with a story.

That is what advertising was during its golden period, the period when people used to say the ads were better than the programmes.

Before then, in the 1950s, advertising had just been bashing people over the head with constant repetition of information.

Then for several decades, under Bill Bernbach's influence, advertising delivered information wrapped up in entertainment, and people loved it.

Then, about 20 years ago, advertising dispensed with information and became purely emotional, a patronising ploy to manipulate people by outflanking their rational mind.

The result of this trend?

According to Hootsuite, in the UK alone 42.7% of people are using some form of ad blocker.

So what's the answer, batter them with more and more stuff they don't want?

Maybe it's time to take a lesson from the longest-running radio show ever.

People are happy to accept information as long it's wrapped in entertainment and stories.

DON'T LOOK FOR AGREEMENT

In 1936, the biggest countries in Europe had fascist governments: Germany had Hitler, Italy had Mussolini, Spain would have Franco.

Sir Oswald Mosley wanted Britain to have a fascist government too, so he created the British Union of Fascists.

They were known as 'the blackshirts', like the other fascists their main platforms were anti-communist and anti-Semitic.

They had the support of the press baron Viscount Rothermere who owned the *Daily Mail*, his paper carried the headline: **"Hurrah For The Blackshirts"**.

To demonstrate their power, the blackshirts planned a mass march into the centre of London's East End, it was scheduled for 4 October 1936.

Fascist politician William Joyce later said, **"I know the East End, it's where those dirty Jews and cockneys live, they will run back to their holes like scared rabbits."**

Thanks to Rothermere and the *Daily Mail*, Mosley had a lot of middle-class support.

6,000 police were sent to protect his uniformed army of blackshirts.

But the East End took a different view, a lorry was overturned as a barricade, 250,000 Jews, gentiles, dockers, and communists turned out to make sure the fascists *wouldn't* march through east London.

The main battle took place in Cable Street, so violent was it that the battered blackshirts ran, leaving the battle to be fought with the police.

The protestors used an abandoned tram as a barricade; the police used horses and truncheons, the protestors used whatever they could find: sticks, bricks, table-legs, even full chamber-pots.

By the time it was over 150 people had been arrested, 170 people and 70 policemen were injured, but the main result was the **'Public Order Act 1936'** was hurriedly passed.

This made it illegal for anyone to march in public wearing a political uniform.

Senior Labour politician Herbert Morrison said it: **"Smashed the private army and I believe commenced the undermining of fascism in this country."**

Historian William J. Fishman said: **"I was moved to tears to see bearded Jews and Irish Catholic dockers standing up to stop Mosley. I shall never forget that as long as I live, how working-class people could get together to oppose the evil of fascism."**

According to the modern Antifa movement: **"This was the moment at which British fascism was decisively defeated."**

The *New Yorker's* Daniel Penny says: **"For many members of contemporary anti-fascist groups, Cable Street remains central to their mythology, a kind of North Star in the fight against fascism and white supremacy across Europe and even the United States."**

That's how the Battle of Cable Street is remembered now, there's even a 300-square-metre mural celebrating it.

Of course, it wasn't seen like this at the time.

The *Times* condemned the actions of the anti-fascists and said: **"This sort of hooliganism must clearly be ended, even if it involves a special and sustained effort from the police authorities."**

Charlie Goodman was 21 when he was visited in prison by Mr Prince from the Jewish Board of Deputies.

Mr Prince asked him what he was charged with, he said: **"fighting fascism"**.

Prince said: **"You are the kind of Jew who gives us a bad name. It is people like you who are causing all the aggravation to the Jewish people."**

The point being, we should do what we think is right and not look for agreement or praise.

Do what we think is the right thing without expecting gratitude.

As Mother Theresa later said:

"If you are kind, people may accuse you of selfish, ulterior motives; be kind anyway.

If you are honest and frank, people may cheat you; be honest and frank anyway.

What you spend years building, someone could destroy overnight; build anyway.

The good you do today, people will often forget tomorrow; do good anyway.

You see, in the final analysis, it is between you and your God; it was never between you and them anyway."